Al Murray is one of the most successful comics in the UK with his alter-ego The Pub Landlord. For over twenty years Al has filled arenas around the world as The Pub Landlord, including London's O2 Arena, and won numerous awards and accolades, including the Perrier Award (after a record four successive nominations), a British Comedy Award for his ITV1 series *Al Murray's Happy Hour* and secured two Olivier Award nominations.

He co-hosts hit history podcast *We Have Ways of Making You Talk* with James Holland and has had four previous bestselling books, *The Pub Landlord's Book of British Common Sense*, *The Pub Landlord Says Think Yourself British*, *Great British Pub Quiz Book* and *Watching War Films with my Dad*.

AL MURRAY

THE LAST 100 YEARS

(GIVE OR TAKE) AND ALL THAT

A Misremembered Journey through the 20th Century

Quercus

Hardback edition first published in Great Britain 2020 by Quercus Editions Ltd

This paperback edition published in 2021 by

Quercus Editions Ltd
Carmelite House
50 Victoria Embankment
London EC4Y 0DZ

An Hachette UK company

A CIP catalogue record for this book is available
from the British Library

PB ISBN 9781 52941 185 0
Ebook ISBN 978 1 52941 183 6

Illustrations by Quinton Winter

10 9 8 7 6 5 4 3 2

Typeset by CC Book Production
Printed and bound in Great Britain by Clays Ltd, Elcograf S.p.A.

Papers used by Quercus Editions Ltd are from well-managed forests
and other responsible sources.

For Willow, who laughed in all the right places

CONTENTS

PART 1 :
PRE-1945

PART 2:
POST - 1945

INTRODUCTION

Before we get started, I think it might be a good idea to
define a few things and lay out what we are dealing with
here. History is all about Definitions, Causes and Effects
and much else, and the very best thing to do is get your
Definitions worked out before you get caught up in your
Causes and Effects, because if you don't define what you
mean by a cause, how can you ever be sure of its Effects?[*]
Not that grown-up Historians these days would ever want to
call something a cause to its face; they're all too nervous in
case there's some other cause they simply hadn't factored in,
like the weather, and the weather belongs to Geography and
that's a different story altogether.[†]

---

[*] It's this kind of stuff that takes up so much of a historian's time, time
they could be spending finding out exactly who did start the Great Fire
of London, things like that.

[†] If you find this book in the Geography section please return it to
History or better still buy it and take it home and put it wherever you
like, to be honest.

Disclaimer: terms and conditions apply

This book, like its author, knows its limits. That's why for reasons of historical accuracy and sanity it stops in 1999, rather than running up until this year. The reasons for this are:

- The Twentieth Century is so event-packed that space could not be found;
- Events after 1999 have not yet worked themselves out to their full conclusion, and while right now it might seem like something is important, it might not be in the long run, and the last thing your author wants to do is get stuff wrong/make a fool of himself;
- The year 2000 feels like last week;
- I have trousers from then that whatever state they might be in shouldn't be judged.

Give it twenty years and we will be able to soberly assess 'George W. Bush/Donald Trump: *who was worse?*' and the like, but you can't see where the dust has settled while it's still swirling around you.

Getting things in perspective

History is all about perspectives, i.e. how you look at things. And like one of those perspective pictures, the further away something is, the smaller it is. Sometimes you can't even see it; it might as well not be there. So, for instance, The Great Depression – which we will be looking at later – viewed from a distance of the best part of a century doesn't seem like that big a deal, but up close to the thing I imagine it was pretty Depressing. (Can't have been hard giving it a name. And you can't blame me for that pun – that's what they called it. Complain to your MP if you don't like it.)

So, no matter how far away and possibly even invisible to the naked eye it might be in the present, at the time it was *happening right now*. It's called the present because it has 'resent' in it. That needs some work but you get my drift.

What I'm trying to say is some of the things that happened way back when may not seem all that important right now but at the time, goodness, they were the only game in town. Which is why when it comes round to it a thing like the ZINOVIEV LETTER* might seem to you and me – with our DMs and broadband and group chats and FaceTime – the strangest reason to get upset and not vote Labour but at the time it was all there

---

* Thrill to the contents of a letter that may or not have ... nope, I can't get excited about it yet.

was and so therefore was *significant*. And anything *significant* goes in the History book even if it seems not at all *significant* now. Or particularly interesting.

LESSONS FROM HISTORY

Any student of HISTORY will know that people like to say HISTORY offers us lessons. Given they have to sit through actual HISTORY lessons they might wonder what on earth apart from HISTORY itself these lessons might be. But there are some obvious ones:

- Megalomaniac men with moustaches in charge of countries tend to turn out to be BAD;
- Anyone who thinks they can explain let alone sort out the Middle East is WRONG;
- France simply cannot be relied upon;
- America may or may not be the cause of everything GOOD and BAD in the world (**depending on who you ask**).

Other lessons from HISTORY (and bearing in mind the length and breadth of the last century includes DOUBLEYOU-DOUBLEYOU ONE, THE RUSSIAN REVOLUTION, HITLER HITLER HITLER, THE SUEZ CRISIS, THE CULTURAL REVOLUTION, THE COLD WAR, THE MOON

LANDINGS*, TheThatcherYEARS, etc. etc., we are looking at lots of stuff pregnant with apparent lessons for humanity) are best summarised as:

1. You never know what's around the corner;
2. Therefore always pack a spare set of underwear and socks.

This would seem to be little more than Common Sense, but if History teaches us one thing it's that sense isn't that common, and that precisely because you never know what's around the corner, you can pack as much Common Sense as you like, but if you don't pack the spare set of underwear and socks, the thing you don't know is around the corner will get you, as sure as egg and chips is egg and chips.

Bias

Some of the History in this book suffers from BIAS. Specifically, my bias. Happy to admit it: I suffer from bias. But then so do you. You should admit to it too.

There are things you like, things you don't like. Some of you like brown sauce with a sausage sandwich; some of you like ketchup. Some of you like neither. No one likes both.

---

* Yes, it happened, don't be silly.

History is just the same – not in terms of brown sauce and ketchup, of course, but there's bias in things you had no idea had any bias. That's why you will see every now and again in this book the words '**depending on who you ask**'. This can apply to the strangest things, even when you'd think it couldn't possibly, like who made the first powered flight or who invented the television and did STALIN starve millions of people needlessly in Ukraine?* Facts very often come along and ruin everything, and only the most powerful bias shield will stop them from getting through.

Often enough, bias will be expressed by the things that aren't given much space in this book, or get left out altogether. Keep your eyes peeled for that. If something isn't in here it's because I am a) totally biased b) not interested, and b) will be because of a).

This may well be the first History book to admit cheerfully that it is biased and Non-Definitive: it doesn't cover everything not because of unconscious bias, but because the author is only human, and can't possibly know everything, let alone be interested in or cover everything. If you've come here for South America or Mongolia or even New Zealand let it be known this is a British History Book, so you've come to the wrong place.

Also, if something doesn't feature it will be because like

---

* Two out of three of these are claimed by France.

any self-respecting British History Book the subject is either too embarrassing, too depressing or both. How will we ever muddle through if we dwell on all the horrendous things we may have done? as a marriage guidance counsellor once said to me at a price of £75 an hour.

Therefore, should you find your preferred atrocity isn't present and correct within these pages that's because History's other main purpose apart from the rigorous pursuit of truth is as a bedtime story, and no one wants to have nightmares.

One thing after another: dates, names, meanwhiles

The thing you may come away from this book concluding is the very thing that gets said about History a lot, which is that it is one thing after another. As a proposition it's hard to argue with it. That's the nature of the beast. It's also been said that those who forget their History are condemned to retake their A-level. Definitely no arguing with that.

But what matters more than anything is this: we will never know where we are, or where we are headed, if we don't know where we came from. This alone is reason enough to know some History, though honestly, **don't sweat the dates** as long as you get stuff in the right order.

This is why events helpfully get given names even while the event is going on, to assist those of us looking back now: the Second World War (WERWERTWO), for instance, was called that at the time. After all, Winston Churchill* was planning to write a series of History books even while it was happening and wanted to get the branding right.

Some events – like THE MINERS' STRIKE for example – have helpful labels that tell you what they are. THE SUEZ CRISIS usefully contains both location and description – you don't need to know that much more about it than its name and you're halfway home to understanding it.

By contrast, there are some historic events that have names that only really work if you have a particularly bleak sense of humour. THE CULTURAL REVOLUTION, for instance, demands the highest tensile ironic strength, or THE COLD WAR, which if you're Vietnamese is a joke that just isn't funny no matter how you tell it.

You will from time to time run into what are noted as **MOST CRITICAL EVENTS OF ALL**. While History is very much in the opinion business, these are not up for debate, thank you very much, and if you think they are, I'll tell you what, you're wrong.

The other thing to consider in the study of History is the MEANWHILE. MEANWHILEs happen all the time, and it's all too easy to forget a MEANWHILE when considering an event, as it usually happens when you've made your mind up about

---

* Churchill Churchill Churchill Churchill Churchill Churchill, Churchill Churchill Churchill Churchill Churchill Churchill; Churchill Churchill Churchill Churchill Churchill Churchill Churchill, Churchill.

the darned thing. Forgetting a MEANWHILE is like when you forget someone's anniversary – embarrassing and inexcusable and completely normal.

Summary

So, in summary, we are going to start this survey of the Last Hundred Years (Give or Take) and All That in 1914 with the First World War (DOUBLEYOUDOUBLEYOU ONE) as a way of getting this thing going. It is The Big Bang, no pun intended. Anything before that is ancient History and/or subject to costume drama/adaptation.

PART 1:

PRE-1945

DOUBLEYOUDOUBLEYOU ONE, 1914–18

The Big Bang (literally)

The First World War – though of course they didn't know it was going to be called that at the time, and how could they? – was known as the Great War once it had become clear there was a great big war involving all of Europe's big players. Reasons for this may seem obscure now but 'great' at the time was understood to mean 'big, enormous, huge'. Not, as the kids might say these days, 'sick', which might also lead to similar misunderstandings generations later.

Having said that, there's evidence that at the time people were thinking 'Great, War!' and not with a sarcastic reading. There are pictures of people gathering in Germany who seem well into it, to put it mildly, and the atmosphere in England in the summer of 1914 was not unlike that of the anticipation before a Cup Final, back when Cup Finals were something to anticipate rather than an anti-climactic formality, which was much more the feeling before WERWERTWO.

If you know about DOUBLEYOUDOUBLEYOU ONE at

all, it's most likely come to you via the medium of poems you had to do for GCSE or, if you're really old like me, O-level. So when you hear that DOUBLEYOUDOUBLEYOU ONE was futile, it certainly wasn't futile from the point of view of people who needed to fill up future English Lit lessons: indeed it was a godsend. The other primary source for many is *Blackadder* – the one in the trenches in case you were confused about that.

Without a doubt, the Great War is where all the trouble we find ourselves in right now got started, though at first glance that might not seem obvious. 'It's a long time ago; how could something that happened more than a hundred years ago be relevant?' cry the dullard, dimwit and incurious.

But DOUBLEYOUDOUBLEYOU ONE is the cause of everything now, and so, like a forensic cop dusting down a cold-case crime scene, we are going to have to take a look at what caused it and whose DNA is all over it.

Causes of DOUBLEYOUDOUBLEYOU ONE

1. **Imperialism.**[*] Everyone wanted an empire, and that inevitably meant bumping into another empire when you tried to increase the size of yours, what with this era (and ours)

---

[*] Imperialism is fantastically helpful when doing History, as it explains everything without you having to explain anything. When in doubt, this is your number-one cause of everything. Save yourself the bother of a long answer. Imperialism is your flexible friend too: it's your number one CAUSE and can even double as an EFFECT as well.

pre-dating intergalactic flight. Everyone in Europe had had a go at carving up Africa and elsewhere; they all wanted a piece of the action. The British had the biggest empire at the time and to demonstrate their awesome might and power they had recently been involved in a long, protracted, expensive and bitter war with the Boers in South Africa that had got no one anywhere much. France had colonies all over the world, the Dutch too, Russia was basically an enormous empire, Germany had bits of Africa and Belgium had an empire in the Congo though they'd done what they could to kill everyone there, as if to make the point.

2. **Prussian militarism**. What this means is 'the Germans', but it's a far smarter answer than just saying 'the Germans', and seeing as there's no such place as Prussia* any more you won't go upsetting anyone if you give it as your answer. But basically this means that the Germans, because of the Prussian Military Tradition, were totally up for a war, in a way that the French with their national hero Napoleon simply weren't, nor the Russians with their enormous army, nor the British with their globe-spanning navy. It's different, OK?†

---

* The very notion of Prussia was deemed too dangerous after WER-WERTWO for being a hotbed of Prussian-ness and was removed from the map.

† The Prussian Military Tradition dates back to the time of Frederick the Great, who was called 'the Great' not because he was big, enormous or huge, but because he did big, enormous, huge stuff. They had a military academy, a professional officer corps and secret plans for invading France, the lot.

3. **The Balkans**. The Balkans were a part of the Austro-Hungarian Empire, which was beginning to come apart at the seams. There had been a war in the Balkans just before the First World War but for some reason that didn't set everybody off, so you can't rely on the Balkans too heavily as a cause *even though* (my italics, thank you very much) the triggering incident was the ASSASSINATION OF THE ARCHDUKE FRANZ FERDINAND by Gavrilo Princip in Sarajevo, which is in the Balkans (see page 19): basically everyone[*] was up for a scrap and the Balkans offered them the chance to jump at.

4. **Industrialism**. The previous century – the nineteenth, so the one with '18' at the start, keep up – had seen the world discover the joys of factories, coal mines, steam turbines, mass production, urban labour, sweatshops and slums. This meant that If and When a war came, there'd be loads of factories to make stuff to fight with, heaps of steel to supply those factories and lots of ships and trains to get the stuff to other places where the fighting was in a way that hadn't been available before. And you know what politicians are like – give them a chance to try something new and daft, and they'll take it.

5. **Arms race**. The British Royal Navy was the most powerful and mighty navy in the world, by a long, long chalk. Any

---

[*] Mainly the Germans, see Cause 2, though I wouldn't want to be so rude as to say it out loud.

attempt by anyone else to build battleships was regarded by the British political establishment as deeply suspect. So, when Germany decided it fancied building more ships, Britain freaked out majorly and committed to building even more. This in turn made the Germans want to build more battleships, which made the British freak out still further … you get the picture. Thanks to industrialisation, everyone was arming themselves to the teeth. The problem with arms races is you end up with loads of arms. And they go bang too, which is exciting. The bangs were getting bigger and closer together as industrialisation and mechanisation came into play. The next war would be a biggie, everyone knew that, and consequently everyone thought it couldn't happen. Even though they were perfectly happy to *threaten* to go to war.

6. **Treaty obligations**. Britain went to war because Germany invaded Belgium, in order to get into France, who were allies of Russia, who were allies of the Serbs who had killed an Austrian who was an ally of Germany so Germany invaded France via Belgium (and round we go again). Everyone had made promises to help each other out, based on the grounds that the promises would mean they never had to help each other out. When the British government did help Belgium out, everyone was astonished, not least the British government. The British had vowed to protect Belgian neutrality in 1839 and had probably forgotten all about it. The moral of this, if one can be found, is don't

make promises you don't intend to keep, as someone is bound to remember.

7. **Railway timetables**. Stick with this one. The Germans in particular were very keen on the railways, and were really into their railway timetables. They used trains to get soldiers into where they were needed for battle and once the men were on a train that meant there would have to be a war. You know what it's like when you have a train journey planned that means you have to change trains at Crewe or York or somewhere? Once the whole thing starts there's no changing your mind. This was called 'mobilisation' and is something that made DOUBLEYOUDOUBLEYOU ONE much easier to start without too much care and deliberation. The Russians mobilised because they thought the Germans were going to mobilise who mobilised against the French before they could mobilise while Great Britain watched and waited and decided whether to mobilise. This is also a good, firm reason to be wary of train-spotters: just who are they spotting the trains for?

You can pick and choose from these Causes in any order, season to taste and see where you get to. But always open with Imperialism; it'll save you a lot of bother, clever people will nod and say 'of course' and that's what you're after, to be honest.

THE ASSASSINATION OF
ARCHDUKE FRANZ FERDINAND

Archduke Franz Ferdinand was the heir to the Austro-Hungarian Empire, which was not unlike being one of those posh people who is set to inherit a stately home that's had a fire in the east wing, the roof fall in and a massive tax bill. They'd rather not take the thing on but they have to.

Sporting an excellent moustache and spending his time being the middle-aged heir to the throne – which is never easy, waiting for your father to die so you can do your job – Franz Ferdinand spent his time travelling the world, shooting big game and worrying about what the Austro-Hungarian Empire should do next. There was a feeling that the empire was falling apart – a feeling based on the fact it was falling apart. Caught between the decaying Ottoman Empire and its glamorous neighbour, the newly unified Germany, next door,

---

* NOT UP FOR DEBATE: THIS IS WHAT SETS EVERYONE OFF. Maybe they were looking for an excuse, but this is it.

Vienna could see which way it might be headed, and also what it couldn't ever be.

Historians disagree about what Franz Ferdinand's actual politics were – liberal, conservative, Imperial consolidator, etc.

– but the truth is the group who set about assassinating him, The Black Hand*, weren't that fussed what his politics were. He simply represented the empire† and they figured killing him would advance their cause of a unified and independent Serbia quite nicely.

The Black Hand got lucky. Franz Ferdinand and his wife Sophie had decided to take a tour of Sarajevo, waving from a motor car‡ and generally showing the citizens of Sarajevo how much the empire loved them. The Archduke had been warned that this was a terrible idea given the strength of feeling about the empire in the city, but he went ahead anyway. Sometimes you just have to do your duty when you're the heir to an empire that loathes you.

100 per cent all cock-up

On the morning of 28 June 1914, the Archduke set off in a convoy that should convince you once and for all that the most powerful force in History is **cock-up**. **Cock-up** is much more powerful than **conspiracy**, every time, even in a case like this where there is an actual conspiracy involved. In fact, this is a good example of a **conspiracy** that was **cocked up** but that

---

* Proper subversive organisation name, that.
† Imperialism!
‡ Cars were called motor cars back then because they were fiendishly modern and brand new.

worked anyway. Ain't life grand?! Apart from what this all led to, obviously.

Security during the motorcade was lax: the police got muddled as to which cars they should be in; it was a Sunday too so there were fewer of them on duty than on a weekday. So far so cocked up. But it gets better.

The Black Hand had sent a team of assassins into Sarajevo to fix the Archduke – and make no mistake they had their very best men on it. Black Hand crack assassin Nedeljko Čabrinović got close to the Archduke's car and threw a grenade that bounced in the wrong direction and exploded, damaging the next car along. It happens. Čabrinović duly took his cyanide, which didn't work, and then threw himself in the river, which was less than a foot deep. We've all been there.

The Archduke then went to the city reception, bloodstained from the other car, and said something along the lines of, 'So this is how you greet your rulers, with bombs, eh?!' Er yeah, mate. They don't like you.

You'd think that at this point Franz Ferdinand would have been hustled from the scene under a cape and put on the first armoured train back to Vienna – a lucky escape in the bag, huge sighs of relief all round and maybe a rethink on actually reading the risk assessment next time. But no. It was decided that after the reception the Archduke would visit the people wounded in the grenade attack, by driving there in the same open-topped motor car as earlier.

And it was here that cock-up goes into overdrive. Another

Black Hand member, Gavrilo Princip, was waiting at a café on a corner with a pistol. As the motorcade came by it paused, held up because one of the cars had taken a wrong turn. Princip stepped forward and shot the Archduke and his wife, propelling his name into the History books for ever. The Archduke and his wife died not long after and it set in motion the series of declarations of war in the manner of murderous ninepins as follows:

Austria declared war on Serbia

↓

Serbia's ally Russia declared war on Austria

↓

Austria's ally Germany attacked Russia's ally France via Belgium which Britain had promised to protect so long ago everyone had forgotten all about it

↓

Britain declared war on Germany.

It also seems entirely reasonable when it's put like that. What's the fuss?

THE WAR ITSELF

Now, DOUBLEYOUDOUBLEYOU ONE is famously the War to End All Wars That Didn't, so when studying it always be sure to remember that even though it failed to end all wars, and in spite of everyone saying it was futile, lots did actually change as a result of it happening.

DOUBLEYOUDOUBLEYOU ONE is famous for its trenches, mud (tons of it), barbed wire, machine guns, enormous puddles and No Man's Land. While this book hasn't got time to go into it in depth, the main thing about DOUBLEYOU-DOUBLEYOU ONE is it was where the British and German soldiers who fought World War Two (WERWERTWO) got most of their ideas.

What were the different sides fighting for? While the governments said their pieces, it was the men on the front line whose motivation is perhaps more telling.

- The German soldiers wrote home about how they were doing their duty and protecting their country from being dominated by their overmighty Russian and French neighbours.

- British soldiers wrote home about how they were doing their duty to protect their neighbours from overmighty Germany. Poor little Belgium!

- Russian soldiers wrote home about how they needed protecting from the overmighty Russian crown, which couldn't lead for vodka toffees (more on that later).

- The French mailbag was doubtless little different, and in 1917 grumbling and disillusionment with the course of the war mutated into a gigantic mutiny that paralysed the French for a large part of that year.

Pretty much everyone wrote home saying they were fighting the war to get the thing over with.

Suffice it to say a line of trenches soon ran from Switzerland (who'd wisely wanted nothing to do with any of this and, besides, mountains are easy to defend) down to the Channel coast.

On this so-called Western Front, things ebbed and flowed in 1914, didn't much in 1915, did a bit in 1916, a bit more in 1917 and went completely bananas in 1918 – that year the Germans gave it one last heave that almost did for the British and the French but actually meant they ran out of steam and were then pushed back and soundly thrashed in what is called the Hundred Days that no one knows anything about nor wants to admit even happened, God I wanted to get that off my chest and no one cares.

The Somme

The most famous battle of DOUBLEYOUDOUBLEYOU ONE is the Battle of the Somme. On the first day of the battle, huge losses were suffered by the British army, which was mainly made up of people who had joined up because they had no idea they were involved in a futile war. Life can be like that when you're taking part in a historical event. You never know at the time if the part you're in is significant or merely a contributory factor to the end result, and usually you never get to find out.

Certainly, the thousands of men who died at the Somme on the first day never got to find out that a hundred years later people would still be quarrelling about what happened that day and whether it was worth it.

The thing to remember about the Somme is that the British army had been thrown together very quickly and that actually Britain's thing was having a huge navy and generally staying out of continental war. The army had expanded very rapidly since its original role as a global police force for fighting the likes of the Boers, and that core contingent had been almost completely wiped out in the first few months of the war in 1914. Having taken on millions of recruits very fast, the army had to train and equip them and adapt them to a new kind of warfare, which had descended not into a stalemate as such, but into attempts to break the stalemate.

Two new things had come to dominate the battlefield: the machine gun and barbed wire. As long as both sides had machine guns and barbed wire, no one was going anywhere much. The barbed wire would direct men to where the machine guns could kill them: any attack going over the top had to contend with being channelled into killing zones, and if the artillery failed to cut the wire, which happened all too often, men would be cut down.

In many ways it's peculiar, given this, that the war only lasted four years and saw the Allies – joined by the Americans in 1917[*] – figure out how to break the deadlock, with creeping barrages, air forces, tanks and combined arms operations. All of these techniques were noted by keen German and British soldiers with a view to perfecting them on the off-chance that such a thing should ever happen again. Heaven forbid! This was the war to end all wars!

---

[*] Largely because the Germans just couldn't help themselves from sinking American ships and somewhat cluelessly encouraging the Mexicans to join in on Germany's side (see the Zimmermann telegram, page 35). One notable thing about the Germans in the Twentieth Century before the two world wars is how clueless they seemed to be about the outside world, which is probably why they declared war on it twice.

Somme salient facts[*]

When it comes down to it though, there are four things you need to know about the Battle of the Somme:

1. On 1 July 1916, the first day of the battle, 19,240 British soldiers were killed. This is, whichever way you look at it, an awful lot of people. Tens of thousands more were wounded.
2. The other thing you need to know is the Battle of the Somme then carried on until November of that year, so it's not like Day One put anyone off. Many, many more were killed and injured.
3. Further south, the French at Verdun were doing even worse *and regarded what happened there as a victory*, proving that old adage that there's always someone worse off than you are.
4. Though it seems churlish to bring this up, the Germans described the Somme as the graveyard of the German army. Not that it made them reconsider, either.

---

[*] That's a pun for our military readers.

'Lions led by donkeys'

Along the line, you may have heard this expression about the British army during DOUBLEYOUDOUBLEYOU ONE.

The main thing is it sounds great and certainly makes it easier for us to feel rationally superior to the people from a hundred years ago who couldn't figure out how on earth to get themselves out of the mess they'd landed themselves in. You know the deal: generals in chateaux avoiding the danger, even though in fact more generals died in the first war than in the second. Like it's a competition.

The problem is the quote – which was supposedly said by a German general called Max Hoffmann, to his boss Ludendorff – seems to have been made up by the notorious Tory MP, erstwhile historian, diarist and mega-sleaze Alan Clark.

It's a handy way of failing to explain the whole sorry business that now seems a long time ago and, if you discount the gigantic global changes that followed it, utterly pointless.

Gallipoli: Churchill* takes a punt

Almost as famous as the Somme is the battle from the year before. (Again, don't sweat the dates; people don't seem to

---

* Churchill Churchill Churchill Churchill Churchill Churchill, Churchill.

think that DOUBLEYOUDOUBLEYOU ONE happened in any particular order – the general feeling you get is 1915, 1917, whatever. They're wrong, of course, but trying to get people to think again about WW1 is like trying to push an immense ball of dung up a hill before it rolls back down again.)

It was Winston Churchill's baby, principally. It's the kind of cock-up that ought to ruin someone's career for ever but somehow – thank God you might say, given later events* – it didn't.

Churchill was First Sea Lord, in charge of the navy, and he was a History fan – he reckoned the best way to win the war was to go around the back and somehow get Turkey to join in the war against Germany. His brilliant scheme for this was to attack Turkey, which he believed – from the previous poor performance of the Turkish army in the Balkans Wars just before DOUBLEYOUDOUBLEYOU ONE – would fall obediently into line.

Whatever you think about Churchill, and plenty do think 'whatever' about Churchill, you have to agree he must have been very persuasive.

His plan involved landing around the corner from Istanbul and apparently this would cause the Turks to throw in the towel and join the Allies. How would you persuade anyone that would work?

In retrospect – and that's all that's really available to us as

---

* SPOILER!

students of History – it was a terrible idea based on a hunch that didn't take into account the realities of Turkish politics: the Ottoman Empire might have been falling in on itself but an invasion ran the risk of feeding into a new patriotic motivation for the Turks in a way that the British simply hadn't anticipated.

Not only was it a terrible idea, it was then badly executed. So far, so DOUBLEYOUDOUBLEYOU ONE, you might be thinking. But.

Diggers

The reason we are talking about Gallipoli is the ANZACS. The ANZACS were the Australian and New Zealand Army Corps – also known as Diggers – who were part of the invasion force. Because the landings went really badly, Gallipoli lives on in our collective memory. The ANZACS' losses were terrible, and the invasion was called off and the whole thing ended in ignominious defeat.

And it was all the fault of the British. Their rotten scheme, their lousy generals. As a result, the Australians hate the British (who incidentally lost more men at Gallipoli than the Australians and the Kiwis combined) and don't have anything to say about the French who were also there and suffered horribly too.

For ten months, the Allies hung onto the beaches they had taken when they landed and little else, unable to get off the coast and get inland, largely thanks to Turkish soldiers being well led (with some help from the Germans), and pretty pissed off about Turkey being invaded. Expectations that the Turks would give in at the first sign of trouble turned out to be nonsense.

Also, just like on the Western Front, there was the whole business of barbed wire and machine guns and no one having quite figured out yet how to overcome these two fiendish and hideously murderous problems. This historian finds it hard to pin the blame too hard on any of the generals during this war because they had been firmly landed in it by the politicians, who hadn't grasped at all how warfare had changed into something with the potential for such bloody stalemate. But then again generals are in the habit of saying 'yes of course we can sort that out for you, boss' in the hope that they get lucky and reap that thing we haven't mentioned yet in connection with DOUBLEYOUDOUBLEYOU ONE – because there's little of it to go around – **the glory**.

Dirty Diggers

The other reason we are talking about Gallipoli is because it is the **Super Villain** origin story of the Rupert Murdoch family.

Murdoch Senior, a journalist, was asked to take a letter back to London for the prime minister Herbert Asquith* detailing

---

* Asquith was the Liberal Prime Minister who got the UK into the war: so much for the caring left.

how the landings had been a disaster; but being a Super Villain he couldn't help himself and leaked the letter's contents, even though plainly that was the right thing to do. It caused a scandal that meant the landings became unsustainable – no amount of fibbing about progress being made in the beachhead could reverse the cock-up at Gallipoli and the landings were called off. Beats phone hacking.

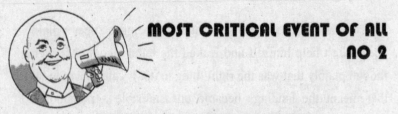

AMERICA JOINS THE WAR

The USA had done what it could to stay out of the war. American politics regarded Europe as far away and none of its business*; and even though the US government had tried to stop trade with the belligerents, the war had been really good for the US economy, with loans and steel and all sorts flowing over the Atlantic to the Western Allies. Nonetheless, two things came to change the prevailing opinion and gradually drew the US into the hostilities.

U-boat diplomacy

- **The sinking of the British ocean liner _Lusitania_ by a German U-boat in 1915**. This focused America's minds on what was happening across

---

* Well, it doesn't sound unreasonable put like that: it's always worth remembering that most Americans had one way or another fled Europe and not looked back.

the Atlantic, though even with over 1,000 civilians killed – including 128 Americans – it was not enough to draw the US into the war at the time. Isolationists and pacifists were able to point at what was happening and make a simple case for not getting involved.

- In January 1917, however, the Germans announced **unrestricted submarine warfare**. Until this announcement, the German Navy had put out a disclaimer that when you took to the Atlantic you did so at your own risk, like when you park your car in a pub car park. For some reason this put American public and political opinion on edge.

The Zimmermann telegram

This was the biggie. What with President Trump tweeting virtual declarations of war during his post-breakfast heave these days, all the fuss about this may seem a little unlikely, but this one intercepted missive was enough to tip the balance in favour of the US joining the fray.

In the telegram, Germany made an offer to Mexico that if it entered the war on Germany's side and declared war on Washington it could help itself to chunks of New Mexico, Texas and Arizona as well as 'generous financial support' from Germany.

None of it was very realistic: Mexico was in the grip of a

civil war, the US was stronger militarily, Germany was going broke – but the Germans didn't seem to have clocked any of that. They'd missed a MEANWHILE.

British Intelligence intercepted the telegram, and once they'd deliberated about how to explain how they'd got hold of it, showed it to the US ambassador in London who didn't believe it was real. What with it being unrealistic. British entreaties and efforts to get the US into the war hadn't worked so far – this was probably just another desperate attempt to persuade them. The British foreign minister Arthur Balfour was wheeled out to show him the original message and the cypher.

Word of the telegram got out – as well as the offers of American territory it included a passage about how 'ruthless employment of our submarines' would ensure Germany victory. The Germans were the bad guys: they were trying to do a deal with an old enemy, Mexico. US president Woodrow Wilson, who wasn't much interested in Europe, knew he had to do something, and Congress duly declared war on Germany on 6 April 1917: 'to make the world safe for democracy'. That old chestnut.

The only drawback was the USA didn't really have an army. They got cracking and their troops started to arrive in France the following year.

The Central Powers might be able to knock Russia out of the war and hold France and the British Empire at bay, but a brand-spanking-new shiny army of pristine Americans turning up meant they would have to do something in 1918, and quickly.

THE END OF
DOUBLEYOUDOUBLEYOU ONE

The war came to an end officially on 11 November 1918. At eleven o'clock. Negotiations had been going on for a while: they could have stopped earlier, but significance took precedence. People were killed that morning before word finally got round that the war was over.

Obviously, dying in war is a BAD THING as it is; copping it in the last five minutes is arguably WORSE.

The war ended before the German army had been fully sent packing back into Germany but certainly at the point at which it had lost. The British Royal Navy had blockaded Germany, effectively starving the German economy of goods from abroad, and the American army had started arriving in France by the hundred thousand: fresh troops who would roll the Germans all the way back to their border and beyond, should the war continue to 1919.

The German government couldn't keep the war going, strikes

were breaking out everywhere, the country teetered* on the brink of Revolution, and even though Russia had quit the war the year before, sustaining things for any longer had become impossible.

So the army under General Ludendorff did what it could to throw the towel in while getting everyone else to take responsibility. Everyone got the blame except the people who'd been running the war. They even got to sidestep the next big thing that happened which was of course the TREATY OF VERSAILLES.

Before that, a minor detour via the flu.

_____

* Always say 'teetered'.

WHEN IN DOUBT BLAME SPAIN:
THE SPANISH FLU PANDEMIC, 1918

The last thing you probably want to read about right now is the flu pandemic of 1918–20. You don't want to know about the hundreds of millions of cases, the tens of millions dead. My guess is that's not the kind of thing you're after.

Yet there are a few **LESSONS FROM HISTORY** on offer, maybe.

First appearing in the spring of 1918, the Spanish Flu was so named in the English-speaking world rather unfairly. Although an outbreak began in the US, news of it was censored in America, but reports of the epidemic's arrival in Spain did make it into newspapers in the States. In Poland they called it the Bolshevik Disease. But the name Spanish Flu has stuck, even though the world has since agreed not to name diseases after places. This censorship made it harder for the outbreak to be taken seriously, as governments lied and denied: ideal conditions, if you're a virus. Governments that lie or deny: **LESSON FROM HISTORY**.

Ideal conditions, if you're a virus

This bit could be accused of pro-virus bias probably.

Those of you who have been paying attention to the dates – I know, I told you not to sweat the dates – will have spotted that 1918 falls into the last year (they didn't know that at the time) of DOUBLEYOUDOUBLEYOU ONE. This meant camps full of soldiers training, waiting, hanging around; transit camps with civilians in them; people brought into unusual proximity with each other. The virus will have done the viral equivalent of rubbing its hands with glee and spreading like crazy. Voila! Another **LESSON FROM HISTORY** – create the right conditions for the virus and the virus will fill its boots.

The war also favoured the virus in another way: the Brazilian Flu, as they called it in Senegal, particularly affected the young and the fit: soldiers, in other words. When Germany and Russia signed the Brest-Litovsk peace treaty in March 1918, prisoners of war took the disease into Russia. American soldiers being shipped to France as the Americans became involved in DOUBLEYOUDOUBLEYOU ONE also helped the virus out. Even though the world wasn't anything like as joined up as it is now – no international flights, for instance – movements around the world were enough to give the virus a lift.

Malnourishment also did its bit: the war provided the virus with plenty of malnourished people to infect: there's another **LESSON FROM HISTORY** for you.

It is argued by some (most notably President Trump) that the Spanish Flu pandemic ended DOUBLEYOUDOUBLEYOU ONE (though it's worth remembering he said that it was the Second World War and in 1917, so maybe he didn't have all the facts at his fingertips). It certainly contributed, but in a 'it was the twelfth cocktail' that got me drunk sort of way. It did affect the peace: Woodrow Wilson had the flu and missed several days of negotiation.

You had enough global pandemic yet? The other thing to remember when it comes to the Spanish Flu is this: while it may have killed up to 50 million people – no one is quite sure, seeing as many of the people who died may have died from malnourishment etc. anyway – the Spanish Flu pandemic isn't regarded as that big an event in the History of the Last Hundred Years and All That. When scrolling through the first half of the Twentieth Century you might see it mentioned in passing, but unlike the wars and Revolutions that nations hurled themselves into during this period, the Spanish Flu gets the natural disaster treatment – not that important; shit happens; you get over this stuff. And that, perhaps, is another **LESSON FROM HISTORY**.

THE TREATY OF VERSAILLES, 1919:
SEEMED LIKE A GOOD IDEA AT THE TIME

So with DOUBLEYOUDOUBLEYOU ONE over with, and victory in the bag, the British, French and Americans decided what was needed was a great big peace conference to let the Germans know that they were beaten and to give them a political, economic and diplomatic slapped wrist. Given the death toll and the damage, you can perhaps understand why. Certainly, it seemed like **a good idea at the time**.

Fact this

The losses? Well, that's something to take a moment to look at.

On the Allied side – and, please, bear in mind they won – something like 4 million civilians or non-combatants died, with 5,700,000 soldiers lost. Another 12 million wounded. That's the winning side.

On the German–Austro–Hungarian–Turkish side: 3,700,000

civilian deaths, and shy of 4,500,000 soldiers dead – and 8 million or so wounded. So much for the losers.

You broke it, you pay for it

You might be inclined to think the sheer scale of tragedy would be warning or lesson or payment enough, but the Allies wanted to warn, teach and collect as much as they could from the Germans.

What they didn't do was send a parade through Berlin and Vienna – instead they chose to do all this in Versailles outside Paris, and make the Germans come to France and eat crow there. Lots of crow. Baked in a humble pie. But you have to remember, it seemed like **a good idea at the time**.

Because the war on the Western Front had taken place mainly in France, the French were dead keen on making sure that Germany paid for the damage done to France.

The victors' concerns were:

- The British wanted to make sure it never happened again – the British Empire had lost nearly a million men in battle and even though the empire ended up bigger than ever at the end of the war, the whole thing had cost a fortune. Therefore: Germany would have to be disarmed. Seemed like **a good idea at the time**.

- American president Woodrow Wilson crashed around demanding that the old European empires be broken up and new countries made in the name of self-determination.* Seemed like **a good idea at the time**.
- France wanted Germany to feel the pain of defeat: the French premier Georges Clemenceau was keen on backdating things properly, and making sure Germany lost the territory it had taken in the Franco-Prussian War of 1870. With France smashed up and a quarter of men between seventeen and thirty dead, you can see why he thought it was **a good idea at the time**.

Name and blame

Central and controversial, though, was the **war guilt clause**: this demanded Germany accept that the war had been Germany's fault and that all that followed from it was Germany's responsibility.

The nation was chopped up – parts of Germany were given to Poland and France, along with 7 million Germans. And it

---

* The Italians were there too, on the victors' side, which everyone seems to forget, including the Italians who got so miffed with how the peace had panned out they changed sides for WERWERTWO.

had to pay big sums as reparation – money, tons of money, was owed.

There were varying reactions to this:

- **Too lenient:** The French military superstar of the time, Marshal Foch, thought it didn't go far enough. He said it was a twenty-year ceasefire, nothing more.
- **Too much:** British economist John Maynard Keynes, who was at the treaty sessions observing, thought it went too far.
- **Way way way too much:** A certain Austrian corporal later known for his fondness for state spending as economic stimulus, such as rearmament and the autobahn, thought it was **a bad idea at the time**.

US president Woodrow Wilson also insisted on the principle of self-determination of peoples: if you recall, the thing that had set off the war in the first place was the ASSASSINATION OF FRANZ FERDINAND in protest at the Austro-Hungarian Empire. Wilson had 'Fourteen Points' that outlined America's principled stance on the war, in contrast to the old-school Imperialism of Britain and France, which were designed chiefly to make it look like what a great guy Wilson was.

The outcome of this was you got the creation of Hungary, for a start, and the once-mighty Imperial Austria was left on its own, stripped of its possessions, like the aftermath of a bad divorce. The idea was to make lots of new countries, not so small they'd be weak, but not so big they'd be strong. Hmmm, clever. So who got what?

The law of unforeseen consequences, signed off by everyone

Again like a bad divorce, someone else got the kids:

- Czechoslovakia was created chiefly out of Czechs and Slovaks (until in 1993 it was split up again due to self-determination of peoples).
- Poland reappeared, with bits of Germany thrown in!
- Yugoslavia was formed immediately after the war and contained Croatia and Bosnia and Herzegovina and Serbia and all those places that were on the bad bit of the news in the 1990s when the country finally unravelled, in a *Long-term Consequences of Versailles* special.

Some of these countries were made up of several peoples, all equally determined, somewhat treading on the idea of self-determination. However, this worked fine until a decade and a half later when these national start-ups found they were too small to be able defend themselves. But Woodrow Wilson definitely thought it was **a good idea at the time.**[*]

Germany also wasn't allowed an army or an air force or indeed a navy, at least not an army, an air force or indeed a navy that would be able to do anything outrageous like invade Czechoslovakia, France, Poland, Russia, that sort of thing. Seemed like **a good idea at the time**. And – even though we don't do hindsight – still does.

---

[*] Though Congress didn't think it was **a good idea at the time**, when Wilson got back to Washington they wouldn't ratify the treaty for him. Wilson's health deteriorated as he campaigned around the country for the treaty.

CONSEQUENCES OF DOUBLEYOUDOUBLEYOU ONE 1: THE EASTER RISING, 1916

DOUBLEYOUDOUBLEYOU ONE is the great earthquake of the Twentieth Century, and it was the British Empire – even though the empire had won – which displayed the first cracks even before the darned thing was over. And the cracks were closest to home: in Ireland.

Now please bear in mind that this section will be too short to satisfy anyone in Ireland, and most likely deliver plumb into the hands of anyone who says the British have neither known nor properly cared about Ireland, its History, politics or people. And people in the UK will doubtless skip this part; they always do. So, best keep it short.

Cause: Britain[*]

The Easter Rising is one of those events that lets you know what happened with its title, though it's maybe too modest in the way it describes such a gigantic moment in the History of the British Empire and Ireland's relationship with the United Kingdom. In short: the British political establishment had promised to sort out Ireland and grant what was called Home Rule; Irish grievances ancient and more recent (in particular the run-around British politicians[†] had given the Irish establishment[‡] in the last couple of decades of the nineteenth century, not to mention the Great Famine) had fertilised nicely into a state of late-Revolutionary pregnancy.

Then came the Great War and the British government decided it had bigger fish to fry than Irish politics – Home Rule was parked. 'We'll get back to that later', said London.

---

[*] Or, if you want to spare yourself the bother of an explanation and naming names: Imperialism!

[†] These politicians, it's worth noting, didn't see Irish issues as Irish issues as such, merely as an extension of British issues they just weren't that interested in sorting. Like a godchild you don't like. Or Norfolk.

[‡] An awful lot of whom were also part of the British political establishment – plenty of people who owned land in Ireland sat in the House of Lords, so often enough they were giving their own tenants the run-around.

Halfway through the war Irish rebels* decided they'd had enough and staged an uprising at Easter, against the British, seizing key buildings in Dublin, most notably the post office. The British†, somewhat pissed off seeing as there was a war on (this isn't a direct quote, but you get the idea), were ruthless in suppressing the rebels‡ and a great deal of central Dublin was flattened. The British used artillery in the streets of the city because they didn't think they were taking part in a popularity contest; they were simply crushing an uprising and they crushed the uprising the way uprisings usually get crushed.

Of course, the British were taking part in a popularity contest, although they didn't know it then. Even though the uprising wasn't in itself that popular in Ireland at the time (what with there being a war on, again, not a direct quote but you get the idea), what the British had done in response ensured that it became very popular, the way things can, after the event. On capturing the main rebels, the British decided to hang some of them and spare some of the others, which made martyrs of the movement and then left the likes of Éamon de Valera alive to exploit their martyrdom, as any politician with an ounce of acumen would of course have realised. It was almost as if what the British political establishment wanted was to be shot

---

* Or patriots. Author's note: you are reading the UK edition. In the Irish edition this is all the other way round: rebels = patriots. You know how this works. Thank you for your understanding.
† Bastards.
‡ Heroes.

of Ireland, which of course it didn't. At least not until things got really, really nasty.

Do the aftermath

One thing, as it often does in History books, led to another and by the time the war had ended the situation in Ireland was fit to burst: the post-war election in December 1918 saw Sinn Féin (not that one, at least not really) win a huge majority, create a parliament called the Dáil and declare Ireland independent.

The British government didn't like this, not one bit, and by January of 1919, insurgency – as we'd call it these days – had started. After a ton of bloodshed and avoidable unpleasantness, this led to a deal being done with the British prime minister, the 'Welsh Wizard' David Lloyd George, which ensured Irish self-governance plus! a really nasty civil war thrown in to boot, in proper 'be careful what you wish for' style. Unable to figure out what to do about Northern Ireland without even more carnage, the deal partitioned Ireland and left the rump of the population who wanted to be part of a united Ireland to stew in Ulster with the people who most definitely didn't. Which worked out so well in the long term.

What kind of avoidable unpleasantness? you might ask. Possibly most infamous were the ex-soldiers the British had employed as auxiliaries, a sort of militia police force known as the Black and Tans, who became a byword for British violence

51

and oppression. As if to make it clear just how much the British were past caring about the impression they had made in Ireland, at one point, in response to British Intelligence officers being murdered, auxiliaries took machine guns into Croke Park Gaelic sports ground and shot up the players and crowd. Because nothing says 'please can we sort this out I don't want to leave you' like opening fire on a football match. And because this is how History works it was on a Sunday and so inevitably it became known as Bloody Sunday.

Once the British had left, the Irish got into the kind of score-settling that makes you wonder what the point of anything is, but fair enough, if anyone was going to kill Irish people in Ireland now it would be other Irish people. The Revolution didn't exactly eat its own, but it stuck a fair few in the blender or under the grill.

The new country, the Irish Free State, set about trying to distance itself from the UK, even though there remained a constant drain of people going to work there and elsewhere. But the main thing was Ireland was in charge of its own destiny, which is what really matters after all, despite being next door to a much bigger, richer and more powerful neighbour it depended on financially. Happy days.

The bit left behind as part of the United Kingdom? We'll get to that. Well, I'll try; it's very complicated and the opportunities to upset someone really are endless.

Effects

The rest of the British Empire took one look at the Easter Rising and the subsequent emergence of the Irish Free State and thought, 'Well, if the Irish can do that and they're right next door to the UK and have a tiny population ...' India in particular. Though probably not the partition part.

Thing to remember

→ If you're British: none of it.

→ If you're Irish: hell, I'm not going to tell you what to do. Surely that's the **LESSON FROM HISTORY** here?

CONSEQUENCES OF DOUBLEYOUDOUBLEYOU ONE 2: THE RUSSIAN REVOLUTION, 1917

Causes: lots

One of the products of the pointless conflict known as DOUBLEYOUDOUBLEYOU ONE – in this book at least – was the epoch-shattering end of tsarist Russia via the Russian Revolution. This was something a lot of people had hoped for but never truly imagined would come about, until the war intervened in the fate of the Russian tsars, the Romanovs.

The tsar of Russia came from a long line of Russian rulers who tended to figure out what they needed to do to sort Russia out a full twenty years too late. The last tsar (he wasn't called that; he didn't know he was the last one at the time), Tsar Nicholas II, found himself in a peculiar situation. The country was so huge and old and slow that he didn't have that much power but he attempted to throw his weight around nonetheless, so he was in effect a weak ruler who was regarded as a tyrant.

Paradox reigned, rather than the tsar. The tsar probably fits this author's Crap Man of History Theory: wrong guy, wrong place, wrong time. Had he been a little less crap, regardless of the constraints upon him, things may have turned out differently.* The study of History often focuses on the people who achieved stuff because they set out to do so, who caused change by effort and talent as well as luck and the help of others. Tsar Nicholas II was pretty much the opposite – a true Crap Man of History.

Similarly, the tsarist state was relatively weak. This meant that the tsar couldn't actually do that much, and whenever he tried to do anything – good, bad, hare-brained, mediocre and twenty years too late, whatever – it would either fail, be ignored, cause him trouble with plenty of vested interests who liked how weak he was thank you very much, or cause him trouble with people who did actually want him to sort the country out.

Unfortunately, this meant when the tsar did try to fix things he thought might be the problem, he tended do it heavy-handedly, which made him as unpopular as he was ineffectual – it reinforced both that he was weak and a tyrant. Round the tsar went: being unpopular made him ineffectual. Being ineffectual made him unpopular. He believed that he had the absolute right to reign but knew that it wasn't possible. The Russian state was like a bell with a crack; it wouldn't ring properly and if he struck it too hard it might shatter.

---

* Differently includes of course possibly far worse.

Tsar Nicholas II had already endured a Revolution in 1905, fending off disaster for the regime, so what came in 1917 wasn't his first Revolutionary rodeo, but the circumstances were very different this time thanks to the war.

The tsar's family, however, weren't really to know, as they lived a detached existence quite divorced from the realities of Russian life and society and an understanding of what their power actually amounted to. (If this sounds like a recipe for disaster, well, that's because it is.)

Recipe for disaster, you say? How can I help?

Russia was a largely agricultural and peasant country, with some industrialisation, and the last thing Russia and the tsar's rickety system could afford was getting caught up in a gigantic long continental industrial war, so when things went pear-shaped with Austria and Germany in 1914, Tsar Nicholas naturally jumped at the chance to get stuck in. Russia's armed forces had a fearsome reputation if you were, say, a trawler in the North Sea, who the Russians had attacked some years earlier thinking they had arrived in Japanese waters.* Otherwise, not so much.

---

* This was the Dogger Bank incident of 1904: the Russian Baltic fleet set sail on a round-the-world trip for Japan. In the North Sea they mistook British trawlers for Japanese torpedo boats and fired on them, as well as each other, despite being on the wrong side of the planet. This basically amazing incident somehow didn't cause a war.

As eager as the tsar might have been to go to war – fulfilling his Slavic obligations to Serbia or some such imperio-dynastic twaddle – in general (and in the privates), the Russian army was big, badly equipped, poorly paid, barely trained and exactly the kind of army Prussian militarism had its beady eye on. Russia entered the war poorly prepared, and unlike the Western Front where things got stuck, on this Eastern Front armies ebbed and flowed and fought vast battles of movement, characterised by one thing: the Russians getting hammered. The first battle the Russians fought against the Germans and Austrians right at the start of the war was at Tannenberg on 26–30 August 1914, and it was a disaster for the Russians. A rout. A pasting. A clear message to the Russians that they needed to get their act together. By the end of 1916, Russian losses – men killed, wounded or captured – were 2.3 million.

The tsar, who didn't know anything much about military matters, took command personally. This is a contrast with his cousin the kaiser in Germany, who, no matter how much he liked dressing up as a soldier, peering through binoculars at military exercises, playing cavalry and taking the salute, wasn't allowed to make any proper military decisions – the German military establishment knew better than to let an amateur call the shots.* Being in charge of the army and clueless wrecked the tsar's relationship with his generals. In addition, being at the front meant he couldn't govern his country back home;

---

* Irony sense tingling!

his wife, who he'd left behind to mind the shop, was similarly incompetent and clueless. Things continued to go badly – disastrously – for the Russians on the battlefield. If this wasn't a dispassionate, unbiased History book that keeps its opinions to itself, I'd admit to feeling sorry for everyone in Russia at this point.

Come, the Revolution

The tsar's authority was also being eroded by the family's association with mad bonking hypno-monk Rasputin. Rasputin was the confidant of the tsarina, Alexandra, whose son was a haemophiliac. Rasputin seemed to be able to stop the boy's bleeding, in between shagging everything that moved in St Petersburg. The court and polite society didn't think much of this; indeed Russian society and the population in general was not happy at the fact the war was being lost and soldiers were suffering because of poor leadership, rotten kit, the sense of administrative paralysis and callousness, etc.

So, you'd think something might happen at this point. And of course it did. And it was all very complicated, so complicated in fact that we don't really have the time to explain the thing in full.

NOTE: Before we go any further, it's worth remembering that in Russia they were on a different calendar to the rest of the world, so sweating the dates gets all the more difficult in this next bit. Do not attempt to synchronise watches.

February (in March)

Suffice to say, the political effort to force change started out as an attempt to get the tsar to stand down, and generally improve the lot of the Russian people by bringing in some kind of representative government. The tsar alienated even the people most sympathetic to him and his family and he was forced to abdicate. However, like Revolutions before it, the Russian Revolution started off in one place and ended up somewhere else altogether, like a badly planned coach trip.

This ill-fated first phase was the February Revolution (which happened in March), and the Russians achieved most of this without too much bloodshed, the tsar having overplayed his hand with the army trying to stop strikers and protestors in St Petersburg. By the time the February Revolution was done, in March, the tsar was gone and the Duma – the parliament – was in charge. So far so good. Crucially, though, Russia's involvement in the war continued, and the Russian army's talent for defeat prevailed.

COMMUNISM – WORK IN PROGRESS

Effects of the Russian Revolution: whoa

As is so often the case with these things, the Revolution ran away with itself, and waiting in the wings was Communism.

Communism had been a fashionable idea kicking around the previous century, stating basically that money and wealth inevitably found its way into the hands of a few people at the top and wouldn't it be great if there was a way of stopping that. Put like that, it seems pretty hard to argue with. In fact, hell, if that's all there is to it, why, I'm a communist – who isn't? Donald Trump, maybe.

Communists though, if they can, will without fail make something simple complicated and they will do it in paragraphs – long, labyrinthine paragraphs – using jargon and lingo that makes even the most dedicated hi-fi enthusiast sound like they're speaking plain English. I'm not saying anything new or original here about communists, it's just it's been a while since they had the run of things and some of the soul-crushingly tedious characteristics they exhibit have been forgotten.

To communists, workers (called The Workers to make them sound more formal and important) are regarded as a solid group of people with common interests, singular of purpose and mind-readable by communists. The Workers should be in charge of everything on the grounds that they do the work. Again, sounds reasonable at first glance, but there's a catch of course – because being in charge of everything involves sitting on lots of committees and being the sort of person who wants to be in charge of everything. And probably not getting any actual work done as a result. Helpfully, communists would do the sitting on the committees for The Workers, whose minds they had read so everything would be OK. Sounds grand, doesn't it? No matter: in 1917 Russia with the tsar deposed, there was a gap in the political market for a single idea that would keep things moving.

LENIN:
THE WARM-UP GUY

———————

Seizing his opportunity was Vladimir Lenin. Lenin was a Bolshevik, a type of communist, though typically of the communist political type he had come up with a version of Communism named after himself, rather than Karl Marx who was the father of Communism. Marxism was completely different, make no mistake.

Marx was an economist who had lived in London in the previous century and had written a great deal – and I mean a great deal but I'm going to try to get it done in half a sentence because sheesh there ain't time – about how science proved that History would deliver up a Workers' Paradise. Sounds brilliant, I have to admit. Marx specified neither where nor when, but living in Britain he probably had Britain in mind. Undeterred by the differences in location or circumstances, Lenin decided he wasn't going to wait for History and would be doing History's work for it – again, what's not to like? Lenin manoeuvred his way into dominance by the end of 1917 in the October Revolution, which of course it being Russia didn't happen in October.*

Lenin was a brilliant schemer, planner, mover and shaker, ruthless and one-eyed in his pursuit of power now the moment had come. His wife Nadezhda Krupskaya also worked tirelessly to get Lenin into position to accelerate History and deliver a Workers' Paradise. You can't fault their commitment.

They had a problem. Because he didn't command a proper majority, was unknown on the national stage and was a communist rather than anything more democratically inclined, Lenin knew he didn't have long to establish himself in power, so he was pragmatically inclined to resort to brutal and crushing methods to cement his position.

A sealed train, you say?

Lenin had been waiting and planning for this kind of opportunity so wasn't going to blow it, no matter how many people had to fall out of windows or die of bullet-induced natural Causes. He did a peace deal with the Germans to get the war over with – it was perhaps coincidence that the Germans had sent Lenin to Russia to cause trouble and undermine the Tsar by

---

* I'll only confuse you if I give you the actual dates; look it up at your peril!

delivering him to St Petersburg in a sealed train. This historian reflects that maybe a trained seal would have worked out better in the long run. He'd delivered what the Germans needed and agreed to punishing terms with the Treaty of Brest–Litovsk, ceding vast amounts of territory to the Central Powers as a price worth paying for being left to it by the Germans and delivering peace to a war-fried population.

Lenin set about creating the Workers' Paradise, unencumbered by the fact they were in a peasant country with relatively few workers as such. This meant shutting down free trade and all the stuff Leninists like to do. Lenin getting into power meant the end of the Russian Revolution if you were the sort of person who had the nerve to say so, and good luck to everyone else.

Leninism: what's that then?

One advantage of naming the philosophy after yourself* is it means you can change it around and mix it up if you like, showing Lenin's wily political cunning right there. If Lenin says it, then it's Leninism. Lenin wrote an awful lot, offering volumes of theories to be interpreted and implemented.

---

* Lenin wasn't Lenin's real name, he was called Vladimir Ilyich Ulyanov, so even though he named Leninism after himself he didn't name it after himself. St Petersburg also got named after Lenin, even though that wasn't his name.

Leninism could mean all sorts of things and did: one minute Leninism meant 'War Communism', a controlled economy that a lot of people in Russia found incredibly difficult to deal with, the next minute it meant the New Economic Policy – markets being opened up and free trade resuming – which a lot of communists, who'd spent the previous few years being angry about markets as they'd been asked to be by Lenin, found extremely difficult to deal with. The genie was out of the bottle – already Russia was politically light years away from the tsar deciding which Fabergé egg to buy.

And unlike the tsar – weak, ineffectual, behind the curve – Lenin's new state was strong, made a point of being effectual whatever the Effects were, and *was* the curve. It could change the curve at will, providing course corrections to the economy that the tsar and his advisers would have regarded as unimaginable and preposterous. Centralised power that had been simply impossible to enforce previously sprang from Lenin's arrival at the top in Russia. How was he able to do this?

Let's get this Communist Party started

The Bolsheviks, having seized power under Lenin's guidance, reformed as the Communist Party, which became the instrument of centralised state power. Authority rested in the party. Orthodoxy originated from the party. The party sought to reshape society, the economy, the family, art, science, industry, everything*, and if you got in the way of what the party wanted – and that was up to the party, of course, and, unless you were up to speed with the latest pronouncements, was seemingly arbitrary – life could get very difficult for you.

One of the instruments that Lenin had gifted the party was the Gulag, probably best described as somewhere you really didn't want to end up unless forced labour was your thing.† The *kulaks* – a type of peasant deemed a 'class enemy' due to the fact they were slightly less poverty-stricken than the average peasant – were the kind of people who might be sent to the Gulag, the reasons for which could and did change, and often overnight, and all of this was enforced with the charmingly named Red Terror. And once he'd shown the world what Leninism was, he planned to export it to the rest of the world with the Comintern, the Communist International.

The rest of the world just couldn't wait, you know. The Allies backed the White Russians, counter-Revolutionaries taking on the Reds, even sending soldiers in 1918, and only withdrawing in 1920. Lenin's Bolshevik Revolution established itself in the throes of this civil war – the war in turn allowed Lenin and the party to justify whatever drastic measures they needed to take.

---

* It's difficult not to marvel at the sheer ambition of it all even at the same time as sucking your teeth and thinking, 'Yeah, this'll end in tears.'
† Hard to be sure but millions of people went through the Gulag during the time of the Soviet era – more than 15 million maybe, but not as many as 20 million. Just as hard to say how many returned. Cities at the ends of the world.

But the thing to remember about Lenin is he was the warm-up guy. The opening act. The B feature. The taster. The juggler before the knife thrower. And he had barely got started when tragically a stroke did what it could for Mother Russia and intervened.

In case you were wondering

The tsar and his family, having been unable to take refuge in Britain, or anywhere else much, went into internal exile. They spent more than a year imprisoned, shunted from place to place while the Revolution decided what to do with them. Fate caught up with the tsar on 17 July 1918 at Yekaterinburg, when they were finally bumped off by Bolsheviks who later claimed they were spooked by the White Russian (counter-Revolutionary) forces and anyway the Romanovs were traitors so what were they going to do? The family's bodies were tossed down a mineshaft. The symbolism of the Romanovs being toppled didn't go unnoticed all over the world, given the crowns of Europe were all cousins. If you were Royal it all felt a bit close to home.

STALIN: THE MAIN EVENT

In the background during Lenin's rule – and more to the forefront towards the end because he had what you might call sharp elbows – was Joseph Stalin. Stalin* was from Georgia (not the one near Alabama); he was short, pock-marked, had been a bank robber, trained for the priesthood – though not that hard – and had been one of the Communist Party's fixers during the Revolution. He had a reputation for being paranoid, ruthless, ruthlessly paranoid and paranoidly ruthless. The most famous quote from Stalin is probably: 'One death is a tragedy, a million is a statistic.' Not that he was bothered about tragedy, mind you. If anyone was going to fill Lenin's shoes, it was Stalin.

To describe Stalin as a stone-cold complete and utter cast-iron copper-bottomed mega bastard would be to do a disservice to all stone-cold complete and utter cast-iron copper-bottomed mega bastards ever.†

---

* Another pseudonym: this one meant 'Man of Steel'.
† You know who you are. Thanks for buying the book.

When Lenin had his first stroke in May 1922, Stalin seized the moment and began to nudge aside his rivals – most prominently Trotsky*, who had run the Red Army for Lenin. Trotsky was so thoroughly nudged to one side that by the time Stalin was done he had been denounced, traduced, fled Russia and had his brains bashed in with an ice pick in Mexico. Think about that for a moment. Who has an ice pick in Mexico? Anyone paying attention thought, 'Oh, *this* is the kind of Revolution they're trying to export.'

When Lenin finally died in 1924, Stalin argy-bargied his way to the top. Out with the old boss, in with the new.

Stalinism: new leader, who dis?

If Lenin was a wily old bastard who named his philosophy after himself, Stalin was wilier still, because what he did was called Stalinism by everyone else, but he called it Leninism. Smooth move. This way, he got to say he was more of the same when in fact he was much much much much much much much more of the same, but oh goodness me it was as if Lenin just hadn't been trying. But by placing the emphasis on Lenin, Stalin could say 'who me?' when things didn't work out. Which often they didn't.

---

* Not his real name either. Honestly, the Russian Revolution is worse than Tinder. I guess they were all signing on.

Stalin set about industrialising the Soviet Union and anyone or anything that got in his way of doing that had a rough time of it. The USSRRRR, while it was avowedly anti-Imperial, acted very much like an empire. Ukraine was starved into submission, millions of Ukrainians dying in the Holodomor of 1932–33. Farmers who didn't want their farms collectivised – in other words their land taken from them and their efforts shared together in a government-run shared farm – were also starved into submission.

Disagreeing with any of this got you Gulagged. As we have seen, being a *kulak* got you Gulagged, what with a *kulak* being the kind of person that went to the Gulag (an awful lot of this stuff went round in circles: if you objected to Gulags you'd end up in them; if you mentioned them, you'd get in trouble even though everyone knew they existed, that kind of thing).

Millions dispossessed, worked to death as slave labourers, starved, people taken prisoner for disagreeing, making jokes, whatever, the army purged of its officers – the party became a separate privileged clique in a society that was meant to be equal, then the party got purged because it had become a privileged separate clique, the country was turned upside down and then back again and then upside down again, all driven by Stalin's taste for ruthless paranoia. Of course, I'm just letting you know this stuff so you can make up your own minds about whether he was OK or not. And, in his defence, the tube in

Moscow is spectacular, truly amazing, like the Northern Line on rugby player steroids.*

Someone's bound to argue, aren't they, and what they'll say is, well, was this all bad? And was he really as bad as all that, really? And by the end of Stalin's time in charge, wasn't Russia in better shape than under the tsar? Wasn't it all going to eventually deliver the Workers' Paradise so it was all worth it if you think of the future? And hold on, Stalin's Soviet Union helped defeat HITLER's Germany so, y'know, was he all bad? Admittedly, this last one is tricky though – as we'll see later – Stalin didn't exactly help himself out on that front.

But you know what, it's up to you what you think of the horrible old murderous soul-crushing, neighbouring-country-devouring bastard; far be it from me to judge. This book is staying out of that debate.

Because besides, it's not like capitalism is perfect either, is it? (See THE WALL STREET CRASH AND THE GREAT DEPRESSION.)

---

* Built with help from British engineers from Metro-Vickers – who made underground tubes – who, once their brains had been thoroughly picked, were put on trial for spying on the tube in Moscow. You can almost admire Stalin's style.

THE ROARING TWENTIES:
THE JAZZ AGE

In the West at least, the years immediately following DOUBLEYOUDOUBLEYOU ONE were an age of hedonism, pleasure, jazz music – which you have to remember was popular and not for old boring people – and women attaining the impossible, like flying around the world[*] and wearing trousers[†] and getting the vote[‡]. New dances were created and caused a sensation, flying to holiday destinations became a thing, advertising got bigger and bolder, people bought cars and appliances, and went to stadiums to see sport; the decade also saw the birth of the movie star.

This sounds fine, doesn't it? There's plenty to like about the Twenties, you might think. You might like the fashions, admire

---

[*] Amelia Earhart.

[†] Amelia Earhart also.

[‡] Amelia Earhart and women in the US, much of Europe, India and the UK (in the UK it was extended from women over thirty to over twenty-one in 1928) See FEMINISM.

the art deco. Sounds like a good time. Agreed. Sounds too good to be true. Well, yes. Could there be a fly in this ointment? In fact, the ointment turned out to be the fly. In order to make this age of unbridled pleasure that tiny bit more tricky and/ or thrillingly dangerous, the United States of America banned alcohol.

Prohibition: of all the dumb ideas

Prohibition ran from 1920 to 1933 and did everything it could to put a dampener on things.

President Woodrow Wilson, who you might remember from the TREATY OF VERSAILLES, had tried to veto Congress, because while he may not have known a lot about Europe he knew that ditching booze was a bad idea, but the Eighteenth Amendment to the Constitution passed and all of a sudden **you couldn't make, buy, sell or transport liquor,** as the Americans insist on calling it.

Like any self-respecting piece of annoying law, it didn't say you couldn't drink it, you just couldn't make it or sell it. Or transport it. Nnnnnnnnngh!

You'd think that after being involved in a global war the US would have wanted a drink, but the temperance movement in the US had managed to mobilise against drinking, and they were tricksy buggers, bringing in Lutheran and Catholic anti-boozing lobbies so that between them they were able to command large majorities in both houses of Congress. During the war they had

started to clamp down on drinking because it might hamper the war effort, then when peace came, they managed to ban booze because, erm, it would help the peace effort.

These 'dry' advocates were opposed by 'wets', who were in favour of alcohol, as well as people who fancied a drink and the criminals who were happy to provide them with a drink. The Eighteenth Amendment and the Volstead Act that followed it fall into that category of political decisions that come along now and again when everyone agrees on something and then once it's gone awry they all vanish.

Ah come on, what else was going to happen?!?

Now: bootlegging, selling illegal booze, importing booze from abroad (in through Canada, the Caribbean, wherever) and the gangsterism that followed it is the stuff we know about. But there's more to it than that. American doctors found themselves trying to get Prohibition repealed because it was the custom at the time to prescribe booze for stress, and as anyone who really wants a drink but can't have one will tell you, that is pretty stressful. Pharmacies did well out of it. Ireland, which was just setting up as a new country and needed friends, decided to shut down the whiskey trade to impress the US. However, the Scottish whisky trade was happy to keep selling whisky to Canada and not worry if the stuff travelled any further.

Thirteen years of Prohibition passed as the country grew more and more desperate for a drink. Thirteen years.

While the expression 'I could murder a pint' is common parlance in the UK, in the US it came to mean something else. The FBI – the Federal Bureau of Investigation* – under its boss J. Edgar Hoover,† got stuck into dealing with the bootlegging and famous gangsters like Al Capone rose to notoriety and prominence. The problem was that in the end the FBI wanted a drink as much as anyone else, and so it became harder and harder to justify the cycle of violence that went with stopping people having a drink when goddammit they just wanted a drink. Al Capone ultimately got busted for not paying his taxes. Account for that, a wag would have said.

On signing the bill that repealed Prohibition in December 1933, President Franklin D. Roosevelt said, 'I think this would be a good time for a beer,' which tells you how the whole thing had descended from a high-minded social engineering project to a great big unfunny joke in a matter of a mere thirteen years. It looks a lot like a **LESSON FROM HISTORY** to me.

Prohibition ended in plenty of time for Americans to get their drinking legs back on in time for the Second World War, which they seem to have fought plastered as they can't remember much about when it started and who else was involved.

---

* Hence the nickname for the US police, the Feds, obviously. The FBI do undercover work except when they're wearing jackets that say FBI in enormous letters on them, obviously.

† What was his first name? It seems no one ever found out.

Who amends the amendments?

In order to reverse Prohibition federally – though some states stuck with it for reasons of bloody-mindedness and/or self-loathing – Congress had to amend the Eighteenth Amendment to the Constitution, which makes anyone banging on about the Constitution and its amendments being unamendable and fixed in stone for all time look a little daft or, ironically, pissed.

THE BIRTH OF THE BBC

The ROARING TWENTIES wasn't just a decade of good times and shocking hemlines, it was a time of great technological innovation and radio was at the forefront. Guglielmo Marconi had pioneered radio in the 1890s; he'd left Italy to come to Britain and hooked up with the Post Office, quickly becoming famous for his transmission experiments. By the 1920s radio was breaking out of being a gizmo for ships to communicate with each other. At this point things get very British establishment.

June 1920 was a big year for radio. One show was broadcast from the Marconi factory in Chelmsford. A bit of opera from Dame Nellie Melba, courtesy of the *Daily Mail*. Nice. Then nothing. The feeling in the British establishment was that radio was for the military and shipping and shouldn't be used for the frivolous business of entertainment. Radio was banned.

Two years of wrangling over licences from the Post Office – and you like me are imagining a long queue and 'cashier number four please' right now – ended with the granting of a broadcasting licence to Scottish stiff (he was from Scotland and he was a stiff – they are not illustrative of each other) John Reith. Eager to make sure that radio didn't needlessly entertain anyone, Reith said that the new British Broadcasting Company would 'inform, educate and entertain'. The first broadcast of music came in December 1922.

The big idea was that the BBC would make radios and sell them and produce the content. It didn't work. Funding mutated into the licence that still exists today – if you wanted a radio (telly now) you had to buy a licence. The company then walked a tightrope trying to avoid being essentially the government's official radio station while covering the GENERAL STRIKE in 1926, making great play of how it was impartial. The following year the BBC became a corporation with government approval. It had a monopoly on broadcasting, which was the way Reith liked it.

Reith had started off the BBC to be sober, stiff and respectable. Comedians weren't allowed to joke about Prohibition in the US or do impressions of vicars for fear of bringing down civilisation. Whenever there was a political debate on the BBC someone would complain and threaten the corporation. The BBC would do flips and twists to try to stay out of trouble and satisfied no one. History doesn't repeat itself though.

MEANWHILE in January 1926, John Logie Baird invented the television, changing the world for ever though not quite yet seeing as no one had made any programmes yet. Chicken meet egg. It wasn't until the coronation of Elizabeth II in 1953 that everyone sat down in front of a telly together and squinted at the tiny black and white image and thought, yes that's better than real life, the outside world. Logie Baird's reward and immortal fame was marked through the naming of Yogi Bear, the fat, wise-cracking bear from the cartoons.

The BBC was all set by the mid-Thirties for dealing with huge affairs of state and dealt with the ABDICATION CRISIS by having as little to do with it as possible.

THE ZINOVIEV LETTER, 1924

I promised you the Zinoviev Letter in the introduction and now, here we are.

The Labour Party were surfing the winds of change post DOUBLEYOUDOUBLEYOU ONE with the newly enfranchised electorate feeling that the Liberals were done. On 22 January 1924 they got into power with a minority government.

Left-wing high fives all round. Can you believe it? Labour got into power? Finally, time for change, sweep away the old ways, bring in the ... oh hold on, there's a problem.

On 8 October 1924, the Labour government under Labour's first PM, Ramsay MacDonald, lost a vote of no confidence. General election time.

Long story short: right at the end of the campaign, the *Daily Mail* published a letter that claimed to be from the head of the Comintern*, Grigory Zinoviev, in which he told his socialist

---

* The USSSRRRRR's special 'spread Revolution abroad' department. Speciality: international insurrection and shit-stirring.

colleagues to foment Revolution and 'assist in … a successful rising in any of the working districts in England'. Heady stuff. Given the Labour Party had had a hard time convincing public opinion via the media that it wanted nothing to do with this kind of thing and that it regarded Parliament as the right way to go about stuff, the Zinoviev Letter was incredibly embarrassing. Labour lost the election, the Tories got in.

Except it was fake.

Zinoviev denied it vehemently, which – given his job was to foment international Revolution and risings in working districts – rather suggests he didn't write it.

What's odd about this one is Historians now agree not only that it was fake but also that it didn't make any difference to the election. The Liberal vote collapsed, Labour's held firm, the Conservatives did well.

So, what is this really all about? Sometimes it feels like this event exists purely to give Historians something to argue about. Some detective work done in the 1960s suggests that the letter … no I can't do it, I'm sorry. This was a fake letter that didn't change a thing, God almighty, let's leave this to the academics, shall we?

THE GENERAL STRIKE, 1926

DECLARATION OF SOFT-HANDED LAYABOUT LUVVIE BIAS COMING UP

Coal mining, whichever way you look at it, is a horrible thing to have to do. Dangerous, physically punishing, back-breaking work. Every time you drew breath in a coal mine you were in danger: of the dust, collapse, machinery, the whole thing. You wouldn't open a coal mine nowadays surely, what with health and safety, and even if you did open one you wouldn't get me down it either, not then, not now, not ever.

But above all, you'd expect to be paid properly for a job like that, wouldn't you? Miners and mining communities stuck together, bound by the adversity and toughness of their work; they were the aristocracy of the working classes though that doesn't exactly constitute a win given the way they were treated.

The General Strike of 1926 was not, as you might expect, a strike by all the leftover generals from the war who now had nothing to do – instead it was a mass uprising of workers against the General State of Things. It surprised everyone even though they saw it coming: the government who opposed it, not realising the depth of feeling there was in the country, and the Trades Union Congress (TUC) who called it, also not realising the depth of feeling in the country. The reason being the General State of Things was dreadful, especially if you were a coal miner.

The British government had tried to iron out the problems with its economy, and one of those attempts included the return to the Gold Standard. As the Twenties had panned out, the pound had slid and slithered in value due to post-war debt being repaid and reparation monies coming in, and cheaper coal had come from abroad – particularly Germany. In 1925, the Chancellor of the Exchequer, Winston Churchill, opted to revalue the pound, pinning it to the value of gold. Like so many things it seemed like a good idea at the time. Well, to Churchill at least. This made British coal too expensive to export and uncompetitive at home. And miners' pay went down. Industrial unrest was the norm and frankly if you were going to have to go down a coal mine for less money, you might have something to say about it too.

To try to resolve the situation, the Tory PM Stanley Baldwin (gimmick: being dull and normal) initiated the Samuel Commission to figure out what to do about the crisis in coal mining. It recommended reform and reorganisation, but also a reduction in the miners' wages. In response, mine owners announced they wanted miners to work longer days for lower wages.

The Labour Party, still chasing respectability, wasn't keen

on a General Strike. They were worried about Revolutionary elements within the trades union movement. Well, you know: the ZINOVIEV LETTER and all that.* The TUC, though, called a General Strike – everyone out, not just miners, everyone in steel, transport, docking, printing – on 1 May for two days later.

On the 3 May, more than one and a half million workers turned out.

Woke Royal shocker

Weirdly, the General Strike featured what you might call a woke Royal intervention. George V, not known for his general political grooviness, said, 'Try living on their wages before you judge them.' Move over Meghan Markle.

A tense fortnight followed. The government had prepared for the possibility of a General Strike and were happy to portray it as a Revolutionary attempt to take control of the country. It printed its own newspaper to make sure the message got across. The army was brought in, though Baldwin rejected advice from Churchill (gimmick: always up for a fight) that soldiers be armed because he was dull and normal.

In Plymouth, strikers and the police played football, the strikers winning 2–0. Miners in Newcastle derailed the *Flying Scotsman* but the General Strike didn't offer much in the way

---

* I told you it wasn't important!

of anarchy: compared with Germany where street brawling and mass protest was common, or France where protest could descend easily into rioting, the General Strike ended after nine days – the miners stayed out longer but in the end settled for less pay and longer hours. The strike had failed and the TUC had shot its bolt, if it was even a bolt to shoot. Mass picketing and sympathy strikes were banned the following year. Mining carried on being horrible. Well done everyone. But it wasn't like the UK was the only place with money worries! Rather than things grinding to a halt, the USA was going one bigger, and crashing the whole kit and caboodle*.

---

* A fashionable 1920s dance.

THE WALL STREET CRASH AND
THE GREAT DEPRESSION, 1929

The Wall Street Crash is one of those events that casts a long shadow, but all you really need to know about it is that one day shares were X-amount and by the end of the day they were worth only about three-quarters of that. All the graphs went down.

Why this happened is still up for debate: that it happened isn't. This is typical for the kind of thing that happens in financial markets, and it suffers from the same problem that matters financial and economic suffer from in general: the moment someone starts to explain it some internal part of you falls silently asleep.

But, and stay with me please, what happened was this, roughly:

For nine years, stocks and shares had been going up pretty

---

* The editors and author will not be entering into correspondence about this.

reliably. If you invested in something, up it went – industry, telecoms, steel, you name it, up it went, you made money, everyone was happy. The stock market's mega-high-tech ticker-tape printed out how you were doing and how your stock was making you richer. Now, when stocks and shares go up it means probably that at some point they're going to go back down again – it really is that simple, apparently. It's all a question of when, they say. What isn't simple is why they can't just stay the same, level off and slide gradually back down to what they were worth in the first place, instead of going down all of a sudden. This is something for economists to fail to explain, not Historians, and they're welcome to it, frankly.

Black Thursday, 24 October 1929

Although in September there had been one lurch downwards, largely because a financial expert called Roger Babson had said there ought to be one, calling it a 'correction' – seriously mate, keep your mouth shut* – Black Thursday was one of those days when all of a sudden the share prices collapsed. At the ringing of the Dow Jones bell, 11 per cent was wiped off the value of American stocks. Again, why ring the bell, lads?

The following Monday – Black Monday – it happened again, despite efforts by the great and the good the week before to

---

* Babson called it a 'correction': would you rather be right or happy?

stop the slide. Big names in American industry had persuaded themselves that what they should do was buy stocks in US steel and, having spent a fortune, they managed to slow things down for the afternoon. We've all had Monday afternoons like that.

This carried on for several weeks with the market in proper panic; they stopped calling the days 'Black' after that because there was no need to point it out any more. The market carried on sinking, only bottoming out in November. This meant loads of people were suddenly broke, and stockbrokers jumped out of windows and the like, such was the depth of their ruin and disgrace.

Effects of the Wall Street Crash

As ever, this is one of those events that affects everyone but no one understands it – like a sort of unnatural disaster.

If a volcano goes off then fair enough, there's lava and flames coming out of it, so you get out of the way of the lava and move away from the clouds of sulphur, or at least hold your breath. And it goes BANG! to let you know. For farmers all over the United States of America, who found in fairly short order that banks were collapsing and their farms were being repossessed, there was no obvious reason – like a big mountain burping fire – to explain what was happening to them.

Aside from all the businesses that had been overvalued collapsing and the whole of Europe being plunged into debt, misery, chaos and in Germany's case the Nazis, basically what happened was the banks in America wibbled, then wobbled, then fell apart (these aren't the kind of terms economists would use but they might as well). Just as the ROARING TWENTIES had seen industry booming, consumer spending going through the roof, and mass production and manufacturing reaching previously unseen peaks, so all of that pretty much disappeared in the GREAT DEPRESSION of the 1930s. Swings and roundabouts. Snakes and ladders. Or supply-side boom and bust, whatever you want to call it.

Fact for today

The Dow Jones started September 1929 at an all-time high of 381.17 points. On Black Thursday it had dropped to 301.22. By the end of Black Monday it had dropped further to 230.07. So you can see the scale of the problem here. Currently the Dow Jones is at 22,137.70 points (at the time of writing). What could possibly go wrong?

THE ABDICATION CRISIS, 1936

The Royal Family has always done its duty as a slow-motion super-posh soap opera, and this episode took them to new heights. This one has it all: a king succeeding to the throne and within a mere matter of months ditching the whole thing for the love of a woman.

'Honestly: who cares?' might be your initial thought, and this is a long time ago so, well, who cares? twice over, but this was the biggest game in town at the time. Strap in, it's juicy (unless you've seen *The Crown* in which case skip onto the next bit).

Here are the Abdication Crisis key facts that you might not know:

1. Edward VIII wasn't called Edward; he was called David.
2. George VI who took his place wasn't called George; he was called Bertie.
3. George V – whose real name was actually George – said about Edward/David: 'After I am dead the boy will ruin himself in twelve months.'

4. Wallis Simpson, who Eddie/Dave wanted to marry, was divorced: the clue was that she was called 'Mrs' Simpson *and* her first name was actually Bessie.

5. She was American. Unbelievable, I know. Different times.

6. George VI/Bertie regarded being made king as a result of all this as a total ballache. His wife, a.k.a. the Queen Mother, even more so. Probably because he had to change his name.

7. Prince Harry is called Harry, Meghan was divorced and American and hell it bothered no one much. Different times.

Background/character references

Edward, sorry David, as Prince of Wales was the heir to the throne during the ROARING TWENTIES, and was living the ROARING TWENTIES dream. He scandalised his family by hanging out with married women, drinking, and generally being louche and appalling. Seeing as, like pretty much everyone else, he'd done his bit in DOUBLEYOUDOUBLEYOU ONE and doubtless felt like letting off steam, it seems hard, at this distance, to get upset about it. But at the time, crikey, they were bothered.

Anyway, as long as he was heir to the throne, his playboy shenanigans were regarded as just about tolerable, and if it were me, I'd have been making the most of the free champagne and intercourse.

At some point in the early Thirties Prince Edward (not Prince Dave) met Mrs Simpson – again her name surely setting off alarm bells that she was divorced. They fell in love and he did the thing you do when you're serious, even if you're the heir to the throne: he took his girlfriend to meet his parents. George V – that's the one actually called George – was unimpressed; he didn't approve of divorced people and he certainly didn't approve of his son falling in love with someone who was divorced. And American.

So far, so tedious, frankly. It's not as if in 1935, 1936 there wasn't other really important stuff going on that the British government might have to worry about. But this was incredibly important in the way things can be even if you think 'well, really??' every time you read about this.

Also

Like lots of posh people at the time, Ed/Dave had expressed an interest in the fascist dictators popping up in Europe. The Royal family is keen on saying it isn't political but making admiring noises about HITLER and Mussolini is I think what you'd call political. And given what was to come, it makes Eddie/Dave look pretty daft.

Stop, you might say, this is all with the benefit of hindsight! But by the time Daveward was hanging out with HITLER in 1937 – there are photos of the crappy couple meeting with HITLER doing that 'Ha ha I can't believe this mug has fallen for it!' face that crops up so often in the Thirties – HITLER had made himself pretty clear on what he had in mind in the way of war and genocide. Ed/Dave had gone against the British government's advice and was photographed giving HITLER salutes etc.; while this was after the Abdication Crisis, it gives a fair indication of what kind of king he might have been.

In a nutshell

1. Playboy super-shagger supreme decides to settle down;
2. Picks the exact person most likely to piss everyone off;
3. Is eyeing up Adolf and Co.

OK, we've cranked our way up to the start of the Abdication Crisis rollercoaster, let's go!

Enough background!

George V died on 20 January 1936 – helped on his way by the family doctor so the death could be announced in *The Times*. David stopped being David and became Edward: he became king and spent most of the year doing king stuff – visiting places, being seen, someone trying to shoot him* and so on – but also putting off making a decision about marrying Mrs Simpson.

HOWEVER: and here's a HOWEVER if ever there was one – the new king's relationship wasn't being reported because the papers in the UK at the time didn't report any of this kind

---

* Oh yeah. The king was riding through London and a man called George McMahon, who could probably be best described as a man hellbent on making trouble, got a revolver out only to be wrestled to the ground and stopped. He was one of those people 'known to the security services', but most likely in an 'oh God not him again' way.

of thing. It was regarded as no one's business, least of all the public's. So when Mrs Simpson's divorce got underway, signalling the king's intention to marry her, the news was reported everywhere except in Britain.

The government got involved at this point. Prime Minister Stanley Baldwin (who had made a virtue of not doing much, really) put his foot down and told EdwarDave – the king, that is, no longer simply the UK and Dominions' Imperial-standard mega-shagger – that he could not marry Mrs Simpson, no matter how freshly divorced she might be. This was because as king he was head of the Church of England – founded purely *to get Henry VIII a divorce* – and due to British irony rules as explained by the Archbishop of Canterbury he couldn't marry someone divorced.

The king proposed a compromise. He would marry Mrs Simpson (how she must have regretted being called Mrs) but she wouldn't be queen and any children they had wouldn't be allowed to succeed to the Crown. Winston Churchill – at this point giving it the full Wilderness Years edgelord schtick – thought this was a grand idea and embraced it in a desperate attempt to be right about something everyone else agreed on.

Then the Dominions' governments also got involved: the Australians and Canadians saying they wouldn't stand for it either, the Kiwis wondering what was going on, the Irish not much bothered.

Push, as it is said, came to shove and Edward had to step down as king. He broadcast to the nation about how he'd been forced out and not allowed to marry the 'woman I love' and the British public who hadn't known what was going on were astonished/not bothered/heartbroken/elated/dismayed/fine with it.

Aftermath

Edward and Mrs Simpson – even after they got married that's what she was known as – became the Duke and Duchess of Windsor. They were stripped of being called 'Your Royal Highness' (this stuff really stings if it matters to you) and settled in France.

When the war began, the duke, who was regarded by those in the know as a Nazi, was eventually sent to the Bahamas to be the governor where it was figured a) he could do the least harm, and b) he'd feel most snubbed. It worked a charm. After the war they returned to France and lived in a peculiar sort of exile, flicking posh Vs at the Royal family. All photos from this time feature the duke looking like he's sitting on sandpaper and the duchess telling him he likes it.

The new king – George VI/Bertie nil – was thrown into the role as King of the World's Biggest Empire Ever Without Any Real Power and embarked on excellently petty and vindictive small stuff against the Windsors as well as embracing the job as king fully. Slights included:

1. Not answering their calls;
2. Cutting their money;
3. Not letting them come back to Britain;
4. Saying stuff like, 'You're dead to me, you slags!'*

MEANWHILE other bigger stuff was happening all over the world and it is to this that we must turn our attention, thank God.

---

* I have no corroborative source for this but it sounds about right.

HITLER HITLER HITLER

So now we come to 1930s Germany, the rise of the Nazis and all that. Not sure there's a lot I can add given the sheer amount published on this topic. But here goes.

Hitler Hitler Hitler Hitler Hitler Hitler Hitler Hitler Hitler Hitler. Hitler Hitler. Hitler Hitler Hitler, Weimar, Hitler, Hitler Hitler Hitler Hitler Hitler Hitler, Hyperinflation, money in wheelbarrows! Hitler Hitler Hitler Hitler Hitler Hitler Hitler, Hitler Hitler. Hitler Hitler Hitler Hitler.*

Hitler Hitler.

Hitler Hitler Hitler Hitler Hitler Hitler Hitler Goering Hitler Hitler Hitler Hitler Hitler Hitler Hitler, Hitler Hitler Hitler Hitler Hitler Hitler Hitler Hitler Hitler Hitler Hitler. Hitler, Hitler – Hitler Hitler Hitler. Hitler Hitler Hitler Hitler Hitler Hitler?†

---

* Hitler.

† Hitler Hitler Hitler Hitler Hitler Hitler Hitler Hitler Hitler Hitler Hitler Hitler Hitler Hitler, Hitler Hitler Hitler Hitler Hitler Hitler Hitler Hitler Hitler Hitler Hitler Hitler Hitler. Hitler, Hitler – Hitler Hitler Hitler.

1. Hitler.
2. Hitler Hitler Hitler Hitler Hitler Hitler Hitler.
3. Hitler Hitler *Hitler*.

Hitler Hitler Hitler Hitler Hitler Hitler Hitler Night of the Long Knives Hitler Hitler Hitler Hitler Hitler Hitler Hitler, Hitler Hitler? Hitler *Hitler* Hitler, Hitler Hitler Hitler Hitler Hitler; Hitler Hitler Hitler. Hitler, Hitler – Hitler Hitler Hitler. Hitler Hitler Hitler Hitler Hitler Hitler? Hated Jews. Hitler Hitler. Hitler, Hitler Hitler Hitler Hitler Hitler; Hitler Hitler Hitler.

Hitler.

Hitler Hitler Hitler: 'Heil Hitler'.

Hitler Hitler Hitler Hitler: Hitler Hitler Hitler Hitler Hitler.

- Hitler
- Hitler Hitler Hitler.[*]
- Hitler – Hitler, Hitler Hitler. Hitler Hitler Hitler?
- STALIN.

Hitler Hitler Hitler Hitler Hitler Hitler Hitler Hitler Hitler Hitler Hitler Hitler Hitler Hitler, Hitler Hitler? Hitler Hitler Hitler, Hitler Hitler Hitler Hitler Hitler; Hitler Hitler Hitler. Hitler, Chamberlain, Munich, STALIN, Poland, Hitler Hitler Hitler Hitler Hitler; Hitler. World War Two.

---

* Hitler Hitler.

Author's note: yes, yes what about Spain?

We take a moment's breath right now to reassure the reader that yes, the story of the 1930s is well worn and that many people have studied this for GCSE, and that maybe, good gosh do we need to go over all this again? And that maybe your mind is turning to the same old stuff you did, like:

Nazi Dictatorship & Control

Propaganda or Terror?

Changing the Lives of German People

The KdF and the Beauty of Labour Scheme

And all that other stuff that cluttered up your mind as the exams got closer. And quite rightly you might ask: 'What about the SPANISH CIVIL WAR?' You might say, 'We never did that for GCSE!' Well, if you've heard of the Spanish Civil War you may know that George Orwell, the animal farming book bloke, went to fight there. Or that the Soviets sent stuff to back the rebels and the Germans sent planes and men to back the Nationalists. And that the Germans got to practise in Spain and that the Soviets did their paranoid thing and murdered loads of people who had turned up to fight on their side. POUM and all that. And Guernica and Pablo Picasso. And you or may not know that the British and French governments sucked their teeth and said oh gosh yes this is terrible we really hope no one gets hurt and aren't both sides ghastly. Needless to say that's all we've got time for on Spain OK?

ITALY:
NOWHERE NEAR AS INTERESTING

As ever this History book falls into the trap of treating Mussolini and Fascist Italy as a sort of adjunct to Nazi Germany – and certainly when we come to the WERWERTWO stuff that's *exactly* how I'm going to treat Italy. This might strike some as unfair – though it's not as if Mussolini was ever fair to anyone, so I'm not overly bothered. Italy's slide into fascism is remarkable for several reasons:

1. The Italians were on the winning side in DOUBLEYOU-DOUBLEYOU ONE, so how they ended up on the side of the aggrieved Germans isn't a mystery as such but it's certainly striking.
2. Italy hadn't benefited from taking part in DOUBLEYOU-DOUBLEYOU ONE in the way that, say, the British had, who had expanded their empire and then demanded cash monies from the Germans; the Italians felt their efforts in defeating the Central Powers had cost a lot and got them nothing.

3. Italian fascism happened first, and Mussolini's strongman antics gave hope to other wannabe strongmen all over the world, even though the man himself was more interested in perks like lie-ins and mistresses than actually shaking up Italy, a country that he knew perfectly well at the time straddled the nineteenth century more than the twentieth.

4. Mussolini – a journalist – slithered from left to right in the political spectrum as and when the public mood took him in classical 'I am your leader I will follow you wherever you go' mode.

5. Italy remained a monarchy throughout, so despite Mussolini's skull-cracking 'take no prisoners' style, his power remained limited.

6. Like HITLER, only more so, Mussolini wanted quick and easy victories and glory on the cheap, because he knew what Italy was actually capable of. Unlike HITLER, he had lousy timing and kept picking the wrong moment, such as when he invaded France too late or Greece too early.

Nevertheless, HITLER, despite his hard-wired ill-disposition towards hot-blooded Latins (etc.), grudgingly admired Mussolini. He pinched the 'Roman salute' from him, and relied on Il Duce (the leader, see what he did there?) as his sort of totally unreliable smaller brother conscience in his bid to shatter the world order. Every now and again Mussolini would surprise HITLER, whom he found tedious, by speaking up and pointing out that whatever course of action they took, they were doomed. By the time the war began, they were locked together in a goose-step two-step: Italy the junior partner, Germany the exasperated senior. But that's enough about Italy, it's not where the action is. Let's go to China instead!

MEANWHILE IN CHINA

Look, it's not that I don't care, it's that I don't know. It's as if when it comes to the History of the rest of the world it only matters when it affects us. A lot like the news.

But basically, Japan invaded Manchuria in 1931 and then the rest of China in 1937 and massive, grim, bloody, protracted war was fought between the Japanese Imperial forces and Chinese Nationalists temporarily aligned with communists that honestly we'd all do ourselves a favour to learn more about but this book has a word count and I'm up against it right now and look, I live in Europe, don't I? It's bound to be Euro-centric, heaven help me.

Like I said, it's not that I don't care, but I admit it does look a lot like it.

'NOW WHAT?':
WERWERTWO, THAT'S WHAT,
1939–1945

ThethingaboutWERWERTWOisalothappensatonce

WhenitcomestotheSecondWorldWar,thethingtobearinmindis
thatlotshappensallovertheworldsimultaneouslyanditisalmost
impossibletokeepupwithwhatisgoingonallatonceasjustwhen
youthinkyouhavefiguredoutwhatishappeninginonepartofthe
worldyourealise something else is happening somewhere else
eventhefirstpartofthewarwhichisknownasthePhoneyWarin
which supposedly nothing is happening there are battles at sea
intheSouthAtlanticandtheRedArmyfightinginFinlandandthe
RussiansandtheJapanesecometoblowsandtheFrenchandthe
BritishMEANWHILEsitontheirhandsintermsofnotattacking
Germany but nevertheless build up their arms and armaments
whiletheGermansandtheUSSRRRRRproceedtodismember
PolandandthebeginningsofTHEHOLOCAUSTtakeplacewith
German Einsatzgruppen going into Poland and killing people

while at the same time the Japanese fight the Chinese but still haven'tmadeamoveonanyoftheEuropeanImperialpossessions intheFarEastneverthelessthewholepictureisalwaysthiscon- fusingthewholetimeandallthewhileatleastforthisfirstbitand let'sfaceitlateronneitherBritainnorFrancedidanythingabout Poland which they had gone to war to protect though if you're hard-headed about it it's hard to see what they could have done thoughtheGermanswiththeirbacksturnedontheFrenchborder were particularly vulnerable but that's not how the French saw thingsandanywayinAfricatheItalianswerebusymakingtrouble fortheAlliesandtensionwiththeJapaneseinChinawasonlyjust simmeringdown.NotforgettingtheBattleoftheAtlanticwhich allowed supplies to get from the USA to the UK and involved a colossalship-buildingeffortaswellcoordinationofconvoysonan unprecedentedscalewhichallowedtheAlliestobegintoexploit theireconomicdominancewhichfromthestartwasalwaysgoing tobeaproblemforGermany.

Author's note

Your author is also keenly aware that when you do GCSE History it stops here and WERWERTWO is left to its own devices. They don't even tell you who wins. The reason for this is that lots happens and much of it is confusing; it's one gigantic MEANWHILE. We will do what we can to remedy that.

Obviously, we can't carry on like this, it's migraine material.

But WERWERTWO follows a pattern; at least it looks like a pattern from the safety of eighty years away, though at the time there's no doubt it felt like a relentless surge of horror, disaster and death all at once.

But the pattern is roughly this:

Germany/Japan attacks. Party on the receiving end of the attack is caught with their trousers down.[*]

$$\downarrow$$

The Allies pull their trousers back up, and after another year or two of things going wrong, gather and train vast armies, navies and air forces, build tons of planes, tanks and ships and dominate and then shatter the German/Japanese forces they encounter.

$$\downarrow$$

The Germans and Japanese, who knew perfectly well they needed to win quick, cheap victories because they didn't have the resources for slow, grinding battles – find themselves stuck in, yes, you guessed it, slow and grinding battles with people with the resources for, hell, you knew it, slow and grinding battles.

---

[*] This happens to Poland in 1939, to France and the UK in 1940, to Russia in OPERATION BARBAROSSA in 1941, to the USA at PEARL HARBOR in 1941, and to the UK at Singapore and in Burma in 1942.

$\downarrow$

The Germans and Japanese don't give up when, had they been fighting a more normal war, they'd have run out of cash and the people needed to fight. This puts at least a year on things, maybe two: certainly, by mid-1943, Germany had lost the war in any traditional sense and knew it, and the Japanese were in the same position around a year later, but they started later. Hence the grim and bitter business of Unconditional Surrender.

Why? Because HITLER HITLER HITLER and (Japanese prime minister) Tojo Tojo Tojo.

BRITAIN HOLDS ON

After eight months of twiddling thumbs on the Western Front, a general sense of Allied torpor and a botched attempt to keep Norway out of German hands, it all kicked off properly on 10 May 1940 when the Germans invaded France and the Lowlands.

Put simply, they organised most of their tanks into one single punch, which came through the Ardennes forests that the French had decided were impassable to tanks. 'Impossible!' they said. 'They're impassable!'

The Germans had chosen to try to invade France at Sedan, coming down from the high ground where the last two German invasions of France had entered the country. The French had built a thing called the Maginot Line, an impressive, super-expensive, high-tech defensive zone to keep the Germans out, just not where they usually invaded from.

Within six weeks, the British had fled, getting out through Dunkirk and other French ports by the end of June, and with unseemly haste, if only because sticking around would have involved even deeper humiliation.

The French government had fallen. HITLER took the French surrender in the same railway carriage that the Germans had signed the 1918 Armistice in, and danced a little jig. He visited Paris – once – took some snaps and then pondered his next move.

QUIZ (answers below):

a)   Does this victory occur because HITLER is a military genius of a kind unprecedented in global History?

b)   Is this because the German army has invented a radical new technique called Blitzkrieg that is beyond the imaginings of other military men?

c)   Is this because the Allies haven't really taken things seriously enough and make every mistake the German planners could possibly hope for?

ANSWERS:

a)   No, definitely not, none of it was his idea.

b)   No, not really. Blitzkrieg was simply a nickname that stuck.

c)   Yes, absolutely. The Allies fell for the German feint through the Netherlands, then ignored reports that there were tanks in the Ardennes ('impassable!') and because their communications were so old-fashioned – there was distrust of radio and telephones amongst

> the French brass – the French high command made orders today for tomorrow when they had no idea what had happened yesterday. The British army had an eye for the exit and wisely so.

If you were tempted to answer 'yes' to questions 1 and 2 then we will be having words.

HITLER, however, taking this quiz in the weeks that followed, thought the answers were:

a) Yes, most definitely, in fact this whole thing was my brilliant idea in the first place and you have no idea how lucky you are to be working for someone like me, you ungrateful generals!* Repeat until sweet cakes at 6 p.m. then switch to:

b) Yes, and because of this brilliant new technique we are invincible and anyway they got the idea from me, the Greatest Warlord of All Time. This through until 11 p.m. then the rest until three in the morning:

c) This isn't hype! This isn't propaganda! I am a genius! The French and British ran like snivelling cowards from my armies, inspired by my genius. You know who we

---

* Especially General Franz Halder, chief of the staff in the German army who, though Hitler didn't know it, had been taking a pistol in his briefcase because he couldn't decide where his duty lay as a soldier: doing what Hitler asked him, or shooting him dead.

should get stuck into next? The USSSSSSSR! They may be our allies at the moment but by crikey I want a crack at them and ASAP! They're corrupt and dissolute and Jewish Bolsheviks, etc. (repeat ad nauseam).

Churchill: as played by Gary Oldman

However, in May 1940 the UK had a change at the top: Chamberlain, outfoxed by HITLER and now out of office thanks to the disastrous Norway campaign, had been replaced by Winston Churchill*. Churchill became PM the day the German attack in France began, but crucially, unlike Chamberlain, Churchill was energised by war, and the crisis as it emerged and the narrow range of options on offer suited him.

By the end of May, when it was clear that France was finished and that the British Expeditionary Force (BEF) needed to get out of Europe, Churchill made his assessment of the situation: Britain, and its empire and dominions, would not and could not do a peace deal with the Germans. His foreign secretary, Lord

---

* Churchill Churchill Churchill Churchill Churchill Churchill, Churchill Churchill Churchill Churchill Churchill; Churchill Churchill Churchill Churchill Churchill Churchill Churchill, Churchill. Churchill Churchill Churchill; Churchill Churchill Churchill Churchill Churchill Churchill Churchill, Churchill. Fight them on the beaches, Churchill Churchill Churchill Churchill, Churchill. Churchill Churchill Churchill; Churchill Churchill Churchill.

Halifax, who had been an arch-appeaser, disagreed. Halifax had been one of the other candidates for PM, so he had to be taken seriously.

The two of them duked it out in Cabinet, and finally on 28 May, Halifax conceded. They had had a face-to-face conversation in the rose garden at 10 Downing Street: no one knows what was said but my money is on Churchill having some embarrassing photos of Halifax, but that's because I'm from a squalid age with squalid filthy grubby ideas about everyone.

It may have been that Churchill appealed to his sense of honour. Or some mucky pics. We will never know.*

This moment **is the turning point of the war** and by goodness I will argue with you until I'm blue in the face and then some about it.

Not Dunkirk. Not the Battle of Britain. Not the Germans getting across the Sedan. Not the Halt Order.† And I know what the young and fashionable think of Churchill and frankly it's hard to disagree with them when it comes to his views on race, but without him digging his heels in in May 1940, **none of the rest of it follows** and you end up with HITLER dominating Europe rather than crashing and burning and trying to take everyone else down with him in inevitable disaster over the next five years.

---

* Get down the National Archive and find those pictures!
† Look 'em up, we ain't got time!

117

BATTLE OF BRITAIN, 1940

As soon as the Battle for France ended, with the British extracting themselves from France during late May and June and looking completely and utterly beaten, German attention switched to how to knock Britain out of the war ONCE AND FOR ALL.

An invasion was not exactly planned but considered. It was codenamed Operation Sealion in an attempt to make it sound amphibious and threatening, but the truth was that despite what had just happened in France, between them the German navy, air force and army couldn't balance a ball on their nose and clap, no matter how many fish you threw at them.

It was agreed that before any invasion could happen, the Royal Air Force would have to be defeated. And the Royal Navy too, but that's nowhere near as sexy as what happened next.

Myth me much?

The Battle of Britain is often portrayed as a titanic struggle between the plucky little improvising RAF and the mighty super-efficient German Luftwaffe war machine. And you know what?

→ That's the story I'd rather tell about myself too.

The Few boldly holding on in the face of the implacable Nazi War Machine, mercilessly gripping the RAF in a vicelike attack that is only resisted because our chaps are better than their chaps.

→ If that's the story I wanted to tell about myself I'm not sure I could come up with anything better. Even the planes have groovy names: Spitfires and Hurri-canes. Neeeeeeeeeeeeeeeeeeeeeeeow!

But the Battle of Britain didn't really pan out like that. No matter how many times that story gets told it doesn't make it true.

Yes, the Luftwaffe was larger, but it hadn't been set up for the kind of battle the Battle of Britain turned out to be at all, whereas RAF Fighter Command had. Fighter Command had been designed for defending the UK from aerial attack. And it did it with ruthless British efficiency.

→ It's not quite as good a story, is it?

Far from being the model of Teutonic efficiency, German intelligence on the UK was really bad – not patchy, not incomplete, just plain straight bad. First they tried to knock out RAF airfields, but the Germans didn't know where they were, and the ones they did know about weren't necessarily fighter stations. Raid after raid delivered not much more than losses for the Luftwaffe and practice for Fighter Command.

→ This is just ruining it.

HITLER had been promised by the head of the Luftwaffe, Hermann Goering, that this battle would be over swiftly because he had the deadliest, most organised force on the planet [continue until snacks arrive, admires self in new uniform] whereas in fact the Luftwaffe was recovering from losses over France and a bomber and fighter escort system that didn't really exist. The sheer number of targets in the UK and the difficulty of how to prioritise them meant the Luftwaffe's force was always dispersed and less effective.

→ This is getting annoying now.

Fighter Command, however, had a home advantage.

→ Keep going, this is good.

British planes had more time in the air to attack or be redirected at the enemy: RAF pilots, if they were shot down and uninjured, would be back on their base ready to fly again by teatime. Everyone else could land, refuel and rearm several times in a day if need be. German pilots had long flights, three-hour round trips, little time over the UK and if they were shot down might end up in the Channel, captured or, if they were lucky, chased around by angry locals with pitchforks.

→ I like that last bit.

The Germans switched to bombing cities, most notably London. At the most 300 bombers went in to attack London: when the Allies got bombing later in the war they'd often send 1,000 planes with hundreds of tons of bombs to deliver to German cities.

→ All right, you've made your point. Not sure the
   British bombing stuff is something to go on about.

All the while this is going on, the frankly enormous Royal Navy, like a very hungry crocodile, lay in wait, sharpening its teeth, hoping against hope that the Germans might try something with the few ships they had and the barges they'd converted into troop carriers.

→ Well, now you put it like that, it all seems quite
   ruthless rather than plucky, yes.

The Battle of Britain is also notable for who else took part in it: French, Czech, Polish pilots, volunteer Americans, men from all over the British Empire too – Sikhs, Canadians, the lot. It was all hands to the pumps once it had been explained to everyone what that meant.

→ Ah, that's grand. I like this bit. I can tweet about this.

The Battle of Britain kept Britain in the war, it showed the USA that Britain wasn't done and persuaded President Roosevelt that the US should provide weapons to the UK in its role as 'the Arsenal of Democracy'. It also helped HITLER make up his mind about his next Big Decision which was of course …

OPERATION BARBAROSSA:
HITLER DUMPS STALIN

Paranoid? Or just out to get you?

If ever there was someone on the world stage not to trust by June of 1941 you could probably plump for Adolf HITLER: it would not take a paranoid frame of mind to think he might be up to something.

So, you might imagine that Joseph STALIN, all-time world paranoia champion 1923 and onwards, would be a bit twitchy about his super-militarised genocidal invadey next-door neighbour.

HITLER now fancied getting his hands on Soviet resources, building his empire, and providing the German people with *Lebensraum* – living space. As well as the prospect of disposing of all the Jews in the East. Previous German talk of moving Jews to Madagascar had been just that: talk. It's Nazism, it doesn't have to make sense.

Once he'd got that done, he also had plans to starve some

15–20 million Slavs in what was called Generalplan Ost to make room for the German Empire in the East.[*]

22 June 1941: size matters

So on 22 June (a Sunday in case you were interested), the massed German and Axis armies attacked the Soviet Union, not with complete surprise – you can only park so many tanks on someone's border without people getting suspicious – but enough that it was a total shock to the Soviets. Especially as STALIN refused to believe it was happening. A gigantic, rapid and blood-soaked battle followed that only ended in December 1941, the Germans having almost got to Moscow. Though not quite.

The Soviet Union was big, really big. It created a military paradox for the Germans. They might look good, those arrows on HITLER's map, but:

---

[*] Like lots of these plans, it failed to take into account that if you starved everyone to death there would be no one left to do all the jobs the German Empire would need doing, such as farming the land to feed Germany – which ran an agricultural deficit at the best of times – and so on. There were big rows about this amongst the Nazis charged with these plans during the war because everyone knew this was the problem, but they had race murder to do too. There you go. It's Nazism, it doesn't have to make sense.

- The further they got from Germany the harder it was to supply the front.
- The locals – who had no love for the Soviet Union – were, as far as the Nazis were concerned, sub-human and not worth being nice to.
- The locals saw the burning villages and hanged civilians and drew their own conclusions.
- This was all great propaganda for the USSSRRRRR, which didn't have to lie for once.

Every step of the way, Barbarossa revealed the essential hare-brained murderous rationale that ran right to the top in Germany.

Back in Britain, Churchill* said, 'If HITLER invaded Hell I would make at least a favourable reference to the Devil,' which is what you might call a subtweet, and immediately began shipping planes, tanks in their hundreds and tons of other stuff to the Soviets with the Arctic convoys to let STALIN know he wasn't on his own.

---

* Churchill Churchill, Churchill Churchill Churchill Churchill Churchill; Churchill Churchill Churchill Churchill Churchill Churchill Churchill, Churchill, Bengal Famine, Churchill Churchill, Churchill Churchill Churchill Churchill Churchill; Churchill Churchill Churchill Churchill Churchill Churchill Churchill, Churchill.

Barbarossa stats: looking bad for STALIN – or is it?

Let's look at the numbers on day one:

> Germany and chums:..... 3.8 million troops
> Soviet Union:................. 2.9 million

And by December of 1941, casualties were:

> Germany and pals:......... 1 million
> Soviet Union: .... almost 5 million

Wait, what?!?! Five million? That's more than they started with! How is that possible? What does it mean?

These figures alone tell you what happened in Barbarossa, and outline in 'one death is a tragedy, a million deaths is a million tragedies' style the first stage of the war between Nazi Germany and the Soviet Union. They also set the pattern for what was to follow.

- When the Germans pushed the Soviets back at vast, incomprehensibly bloody cost, the Soviets plugged the gap. They found more people and held the Germans up. Simple. Blitzkrieg was meant to be quick: achieve its objectives fast, knock over the other side and make them concede. As long as the Soviets could find another million here, another million there, they were able to hold up the Germans.

- Motivating Soviet citizens, as possibly ambivalent as they might have been about the miraculous good fortune of living in the USSR, was made far easier by the Germans and their allies torching villages, rounding up people for execution and being generally horribly murderous.
- PLUS! NKVD (Soviet political enforcers) made sure that anyone who decided that fighting the Germans wasn't for them could meet a grisly end.

The Soviets reorganised and, despite colossal losses, cities falling, whole armies being taken prisoner (armies that the Germans then starved to death), they fought back.

HITLER dithered as the campaign progressed and this probably stopped him from getting to Moscow. And, as ever, the sheer scale of the whole enterprise is boggling. There was a 1,800-mile front; 800,000 horses in the German advance; hundreds of miles advanced.

By the end of it, having failed to take Moscow, HITLER sacked Field Marshal von Brauchitsch for messing the campaign up, and got in a true expert as his replacement: himself.

Alsohappeningatthesametime

Alsohappening at the same time, there's fighting in North Africa where the British, Australian, New Zealand and Indian army troops are fighting the Italians who have in the meantime been bailed out by the Germans, who have in the process taken Greece, Yugoslavia and Crete but crucially not Malta, while British troops have evicted Vichy French troops from various African strongholds as well as fighting the Italians in East Africa and dealing with Syria and Palestine (as was) and Iraq and where it was essential to make sure a pro-German uprising got squashed while at the same time making sure that whatever the Japanese decided to do next beyond China didn't disrupt the war effort in the Middle East and the West, the most important part of which was without a shadow of a doubt the Battle of the Atlantic because without shipping being able to make its way around the world safely the British and later the Allies wouldn't stand a chance, especially given the sheer amount of stuff the British and later the USA were sending to the Soviets once the Soviets found themselves fighting the Germans. At the same time, convoys shipping supplies to the UK (mainly) as well as around the Cape to North Africa and beyond continued, with the Allies tightening their grip on the U-boats and using colossal naval power to dominate the war from an operational perspective and exploit their industrial and economic might.

PEARL HARBOR

If you've seen the film, the one with Ben Affleck in it, you'll need to read this next bit. If you haven't you're probably OK and know what happened.

The attack on Pearl Harbor on 7 December 1941 – A Day That Lives in Infamy – is a classic example of the pattern of WERWERTWO, in which the Allies were caught with their pants thoroughly all the way down. They then pulled up their pants and, in this case, it eventually became pretty clear that the Japanese had bitten off more than they could chew. In America's pants.[*]

The USA, under POTUS FDR, had done everything it could to stay out of WERWERTWO, while at the same time doing everything it could to take part in WERWERTWO. The war with Germany, that is. While providing ships and planes and rifles and tanks to the British, the Americans definitely weren't interested in getting involved. The attitude was: 'No, sir. No

___
[*] ABANDON METAPHOR!

thank you. Not after that last one. And how many bombers would you like to buy?'

Why? Japan, why?

Americans, looking to the Pacific, were beginning to wonder just what it was the Japanese wanted exactly. If only there had been some clues. Japan had been in the grip of a militarist fascist (HOUSE!) nationalist expansionist wannabe Imperialist (BINGO!) government for longer even than Germany, and had shown ruthless brutality in China and a tendency to regard military force as the solution to most of its problems.

America didn't have an empire as such – of course not, the Americans don't do empire – but the Philippines at that time … well, look, how do we put this … erm, not a colony as such but oh God look it's called the American Insular Government and anyway that's not the point.

But the US, and Britain, France and the Netherlands, all had what were called possessions in the Far East that they wanted to hang onto* (though by the end of 1941, the French possessions technically belonged to Vichy France).

Japan, short on raw materials/fancying a slice of the Imperialist pie, felt constrained and – being expansionist – decided to expand. And being militarist, they did it with the military.

---

* Imperialism.

Japan and the US had been engaged in talks during 1941 to try to figure out how to rub along: these talks had broken down.

The plan

The Japanese decided – like the Germans – that what they needed to do was knock out their opponents quickly. Because that was all they were actually capable of. A long war would be too tricky to fight. Avoid a long war at all costs. Whatever you do, don't get caught up in a long war.

Of course, the best way to do that would have been to have avoided a war, but when you're a BINGO government like the Japanese government in 1941 you have no other options.

Pearl Harbor – in Honolulu, Hawaii – was the home of the US navy's Pacific Fleet. The Japanese conceived a surprise attack on the base by their own aircraft carrier fleet, attacking and destroying American vessels, which would knock the US out of the war and allow Japan to pursue its aims throughout the Far East.

As long as they got the aircraft carriers, they'd get the head start they needed and would knock America out of the Pacific War no problem once and for all.* You betcha.

---

* It's a feature, not a bug, as the youngsters say, that being a militarist fascist (HOUSE!) nationalist expansionist wannabe Imperialist (BINGO!) government involves a big slice of wishful thinking. And it is often bundled up neatly with a fatal misreading of your intended opponents.

Surprise! It's the Japanese navy!

Operation AI was the brainchild of Admiral Yamamoto. He had studied the British surprise attack on the Italian navy at Taranto the year before and decided that surprise was of the essence. The Americans repaid him later in the war when they found out where his plane was and sent a squadron to shoot him down, which was also a surprise.

The Japanese carrier fleet achieved what the military call 'complete surprise' (which is the same as complete surprise for the rest of us) by attacking on a Sunday when the Americans had their radar switched on but the men had never seen a large formation before so didn't realise what it was. And not only that, they attacked at ten to eight in the morning, when lie-ins were occurring.

Three hundred and fifty-three aircraft swept down in two waves to pounce on the Pacific Fleet, sunk four of the eight battleships in harbour (that's how you spell harbour, btw) and sank and damaged a further three destroyers, three cruisers and a minelayer. Two and a half thousand Americans were killed.

The Japanese smashed up the naval base, destroyed 188 aircraft and then declared war on America. Because the declaration didn't get to the USA until the following day (and these things matter when hundreds of attack aircraft turn up unannounced and shoot up whatever they can), the Pearl Harbor attack counted as a war crime. Yikes.

But: the aircraft carriers weren't there. The *Enterprise*, *Lexington* and *Saratoga* were elsewhere. And – apart from the USS *Arizona* – the battleships sunk were in shallow water and recoverable. Japan had roused the sleeping giant and stirred the dormant metaphor from its clichéd slumber.

It was a day that would 'live in infamy', said President FD 'FDR' Roosevelt. In other words, Japan was going to cop it.

Japan was now at war with America. FDR had now got into a war, but not the one he had been eyeing up. And then:

HITLER DECLARES WAR ON AMERICA

1942: Starts badly for the Allies, ends pretty well

Germany vs USSSRRR

The Germans tried again again to knock the USRRRR-RRRRRR out of the war. Huge battles, bigger even than the height of Barbarossa, finally devolved into a battle for the city on the Volga called Stalingrad, because rather than try to take out Moscow the Germans settled on going south and getting to the Caucasus and the oil there. Not that they had any practical means of getting the oil back to Germany, but let's not get bogged down in the wishful thinking on offer. It's not like they did.

HITLER, never one to miss a chance to make things personal, couldn't resist Stalingrad. STALIN took it both personally and as an opportunity. STALIN's forces triumphed in an epic encirclement of the city and the Axis armies around it.

The cost to the Soviets was colossal, but the Germans lost an entire army in Stalingrad in February of 1943. Another one of those encounters when more than a million perished and, although they won, more on the Soviet side died.

MEANWHILE Germany vs British Empire, and USA, who HITLER had invited to the party for some reason known only to himself but by now I have surely made it plain his judgement was terrible

Fighting in North Africa horizontally yoyoed backwards and forwards across Egypt and Libya. The Afrika Korps, with Erwin Rommel in command, hyped by – of all people – the British press as the wily 'Desert Fox', kept defeating the British Eighth Army.

A series of desert battles went badly for the British. Tobruk fell to the Germans, and embarrassment hung heavy over the Eighth Army – it looked like the British army simply couldn't fight; its generals appeared clueless. The British retreated to a railway station at El Alamein, where the desert to the south was impassable (actually impassable, not like the Ardennes) and the Germans would be forced to fight through to Alexandria if they wanted to get to the Suez Canal and topple the British Empire in the Middle East.

With lots of shiny new stuff from the Americans and a vigorous, annoying, self-confident, pushy new general, Bernard 'Monty' Montgomery, the Eighth Army defeated Rommel's men at El Alamein in late October 1942. Rommel headed east towards the British and American forces that landed in Morocco and Tunisia at the same time. By May 1943, a quarter of a million German troops, meat-in-the-sandwich style, had been captured and the Germans ejected from North Africa.

Had this been a war like wars used to be, the Germans would have realised they were done and sued for peace. But they didn't.

Why? Because HITLER HITLER HITLER.

There's a MEANWHILE, too:

Japan vs Rest of the world

Japan had a better 1942 than the Germans, seizing Burma, the Philippines, the Dutch East Indies, Hong Kong, Malaya and, most spectacularly, Singapore in a humiliating defeat for the British; General Percival surrendered the base with 80,000 men going on to the hell of being prisoners of war, while the Japanese lost about a thousand men in all. This defeat spelled game over for the British Empire; with the Japanese threatening India too, time was up for London's global influence.

However, in June 1942, the Japanese had the worst five minutes of the war at the Battle of Midway, when again they were trying to do something about the US navy's aircraft carriers. An attempt to lure the Americans to battle worked, but in between attacks US navy planes spotted the Japanese carrier fleet, attacked it, and for the loss of one of their own aircraft carriers, sank four Japanese aircraft carriers. Given America's industrial potential in comparison to Japan's, this did for the Japanese navy in the Pacific.

1943 Starts well for the Allies, ends pretty badly for the Axis

Japan vs Rest of the world

The US began to take on the Japanese wherever they found them scattered throughout the Pacific and elsewhere – the Solomon Islands, New Guinea, the Marshall Islands. The Japanese refused to give their lives cheaply and wouldn't be taken prisoner. Anyone they took prisoner could expect a grisly end. American submarines started to sink Japanese shipping in large numbers.

Huge battles in China too. But you'll never read about that in a book in this country.

Germany vs USSSSSRR

Further disasters for Germany: at a place called Kursk on the Eastern Front, the Germans tried to straighten out their lines to make them easier to defend and the Soviets overwhelmed them, though again at great cost, bottomless-pit style.

> ## Germany (and Italy, for a bit,
> ## but let's not go mad, eh?) vs Western Allies
>
> British and American bombers stepped up their attempts to destroy German industry/kill civilians/de-house the population/precision bomb [delete according to taste] and in July 1943 destroyed Hamburg in a firestorm.
>
> British and American soldiers invaded Sicily and then Italy. The Italians changed sides. Which brings us to:

An important thing to bear in mind about WERWERTWO

The Italians, who may have had a fascist government but weren't necessarily stupid, changed sides in 1943 for one simple reason. They knew that by the middle of 1943 the war in Europe at least was lost. It was only a matter of time and an awful lot of bloodshed before the war ended and they really couldn't carry on.

So why another two years of what had now become an apparently futile struggle? HITLER HITLER HITLER. He wanted to conquer the world or die trying, though of course what with him being the all-important leader it was other people who would have to do the dying.

And there was another front in the war that he wanted to make sure went Germany's way, a front that was worth – to HITLER and his fellow Nazi ideologues – all the fighting elsewhere, all the soldiers, men, women and children killed: the war against the Jews.

THE HOLOCAUST

Six million Jews murdered.

Five million other people, too: Poles, Soviets, disabled people, gay people, Sinti and Roma. Whoever the Nazi state decided didn't fit, weren't worth keeping alive, or who, in their view, most definitely needed to be murdered.

Not much more your author can offer on this.

D-DAY AND THE LAST ELEVEN MONTHS: HOW HARD CAN IT BE?

―――――

1944: Starts well for the Allies, ends well for the Allies

This won't fit in a box.

The Normandy landings, a.k.a. D-Day, 6 June 1944 – delayed by a day because of bad weather as any middle-aged man in matching red face and trousers will tell you – was the beginning of the invasion of Europe. Or at least of mainland Europe if you don't count Italy as part of Europe which it seems a lot of people don't.

The sheer scale of the invasion is mind-boggling. It makes you wonder why, if the British state could organise a thing like this, what exactly is the problem with collecting your bins on the usual day of the week of a bank holiday?!

Before we get into the number of soldiers (which is bonkers, trust me), have a stiff drink and think about the spreadsheets that you'd need to make up and look at, the meetings you'd need to go to, the flipboards, flow charts, the emails you'd have to answer, the Google map links you'd need to send to get this lot to turn up on time and in the right place.

And of course there was none of that modern meeting stuff: they did this with typewriters and slide rules* and telegrams†. And where's my resident's parking permit? How hard is it?

So: how many ships? In total, 6,939 vessels: 1,213 warships, 4,126 landing craft of various types, 736 ancillary craft, and 864 merchant vessels. Something like 200,000 personnel. Think of the sandwiches and the cups of tea. So why can't I get a train to Manchester that runs on time and a decent seat for less than two hundred and fifty quid?!

The Germans had fewer emails to reply to, with about a hundred boats in the vicinity. Fewer sandwiches to make as well.

The build-up

The Allies planned to land in Normandy rather than at Calais, which is that much closer to Britain, and to convince the Germans that even though they had landed at Normandy they might still invade via Calais. Operation Bodyguard was the deception plan: a fake army was created, sending itself radio messages, and larger-than-life General George Patton was put in charge of the ghost army. To add to the deception, the whole of the

---

* No one knows what these are, don't worry.

† Unless you're turning 100, these either.

northern French coast – its railway lines, gun emplacements, defences – was bombed, so as to not give away where the landings might come.

Because the Allies knew they'd need a port they decided it was easier to build one and assemble it on two of the Normandy beaches. This Mulberry Harbour is, again, mind-boggling, if only because it was an engineering project that was delivered on time: there was a war on, I suppose. More than 400 components had to be towed from all over the UK and the parts started to arrive to be assembled on the evening of D-Day. THEN WHY IS THE M25 CLOSED BETWEEN JUNCTIONS 6 AND 9 ANTI-CLOCKWISE??????

The Allies practised like mad, training entire armies for the landings as well as bringing men back from Italy to join the invasion. The Germans, unsure of where the landings might be, and caught in their own chaotic leadership structure – HITLER liked to make sure there were at least two people doing every important job conceivable so they'd compete with one another and not him – couldn't decide how they'd respond: whether it was best to attack the beaches or build up their forces and then strike.

They were also expecting an attack by the Soviets in the east, an attack that would probably be enormous and ferocious, because that was how the Soviets liked to do things; and that's exactly what they got on 23 June, Operation Bagration, a gigantic million-and-a-half-men extravaganza, that swept the Germans all the way from Belarus back to Warsaw and destroyed the Germans' Army Group Centre. The Germans had lost the war all over again. This operation always gets overlooked and that's what we're going to do right now.

The plan and the outcome

The plan was to land all along the Norman coast on five beaches: two British, one Canadian and two American. At either end of this beachhead, paratroopers and other crazy men in gliders* landed at the dead of night to capture vital road links that connected the beaches to inland. This all went pretty much as expected if not exactly to plan, unless your thing is reading super-nitpicky books about this kind of thing, and boy, they exist; I've read a few so that you don't have to.

Then came the Battle of Normandy. The big idea was that at the British end of the lodgement, in the east, nearest Germany, the British would soak up (fight, in other words) the German tanks and main effort while the Americans would build up (fight, in other words) in the west, until the Americans (by fighting) would be able to break out where there were fewer Germans (to fight) and with any luck (luck created by fighting) the Germans would be overwhelmed and beaten (via fighting). Given that the Germans were really into fighting and their bosses wanted them to fight this meant an awful lot of fighting.

---

* If you can't call paratroopers nuts what can you call them?

The Allies not only had control of the seas but also of the sky, so the Germans found moving around in daylight difficult – if they tried to bring their tanks and troops forward, they were usually attacked. Their codes had been cracked too, famously by Benedict Cumberbatch with a computer he'd built thanks to banging his fist on Mark Strong's desk and saying, 'No, you listen to me, I'm a tortured genius!' so the Allies had a pretty good idea of what the Germans were up to.

By the end of the Battle of Normandy (fighting!), the German army was caught in a trap it had enthusiastically hurled itself into: a counter-attack west towards Mortain ordered by HITLER had pushed German forces further into the Allied maw at Falaise. Had it been a war like the wars that had gone before, the fleeing, shattered German army's government would have sued for peace and that would have been that. The Germans had lost the war all over again.

However – and you know this by now: HITLER HITLER HITLER.

HITLER's armies were bound to him by an oath of loyalty. HITLER was set on going down in flames.

After Paris fell in August, the war moved swiftly to the German border. The Allies, at the end of their supply train – and expecting as well they might that the Germans would soon surrender – tried to hop into Germany via the Dutch bridges at Eindhoven, Nijmegen and Arnhem. This operation failed because the Germans seemed to have no idea they were defeated. Certainly the assassination attempt on HITLER in

July* had made the Nazis tighten up how they dealt with defeatism and dissent, but their men fought on as though, somehow, they might be able to extract the country from destruction, though destruction was exactly what HITLER had in mind anyway.

With the front settling down on the German border, the Germans spent the winter starving out the Dutch, and as a Christmas special, tried to force their way through the Americans in the Ardennes (impassable!) in what became known as the Battle of the Bulge. It was pointless and costly.

The rest of the war was a grim and grisly business. German soldiers refused to give their lives cheaply until the end, even if their armies had disintegrated. Meanwhile, Allied bombers continued to flatten German cities, most notoriously Dresden but also all over the country – at Pforzheim nearly a third of the town's population died but no one seems to have heard of Pforzheim – pretty much at will. Still Germany wouldn't quit. Why? Because: you know.

The Western Allies, once they were across the Rhine, with an eye to the war in Japan and the casualties they expected to take invading the Japanese home islands, decided to leave Berlin to the Soviets. And very sensibly too: the Soviets amassed another gigantic army – two actually – that like an enormous pair of jaws closed in on the German capital, and burrowed through the city to meet in the middle.

---

* Tom Cruise: failed to kill HITLER, some hero.

Goodbye: HITLER HITLER HITLER

At the centre of Berlin was the Führerbunker, with HITLER and his remaining cronies in it. HITLER spent his time deciding how he would finally overthrow the Allies even as they smashed up his country and its capital. He took a moment of comfort from the death of President Roosevelt on 12 April, and when that didn't change the course of the war as he said it would, he decided the German people had failed him and ruined their chance to defeat the Jews (of course) once and for all, and he blew his brains out next to his brand new wife as she took cyanide. Anyone who tells you otherwise is fooling no one but themselves.

His death broke the spell over Germany and the Germans. Surrenders were signed by the different armies. The war in Europe was over. But the war with Japan was yet to be settled.

'Not necessarily to Japan's advantage'

Japan was dying hard: wherever the Allies fought the Japanese it was incredibly costly, for both sides and anyone caught in between.

An invasion of Japan would be the only way to end it, it seemed. Instead the Americans had something up their sleeves: the atomic bomb.

The Manhattan Project, as it was known, was the Allied – American mainly but with some Brits along for the ride as well as some Soviet spies for good measure – 'build an atom bomb ASAP' project. The British project, called 'Tube Alloys', had been underway since the start of the war but was simply too expensive.

Roosevelt, who had had a letter from Einstein in 1939 urging him to build the thing before the Germans did, got into the A-bomb-developing business in a no-expense-spared way, the plan being to have it ready to drop on Germany. It cost $2 billion but these were 1940s billions so put a nought on the end at the very least. It was super-secret so the Soviets knew all about it.

The first A-bomb wasn't tested until 16 July 1945, only a few weeks before it was used on Hiroshima. The test hadn't been without drama: as well as not quite being sure if the thing would work and how big an explosion it would yield, one of the physicists involved got the scientists on site to place bets as to whether the bomb would set fire to the atmosphere and destroy the planet.

So the US had the atom bomb, and not only that they had built a bomber, the B-29 – at similar vast cost – to deliver it, so the chances they wouldn't use it were slender.

So why did they? And the thing is, here we are wrestling with hindsight because nuclear weapons are without doubt a BAD THING. Everyone agrees on that.

However: the Americans – now led by President Truman

– were facing casualty projections for the invasion of the Japanese home islands that were cataclysmic. The Japanese Cabinet's demand that Japanese soldiers, men, women and children try to take as many Americans with them as they could had clearly been heard: the Battle of Okinawa in April 1945 had cost the Americans 20,000 men in two and a half months – maybe half the island's Japanese population of 300,000 were killed or committed suicide.

The atom bomb offered the Americans the possibility of beating the Japanese; the US had shown plenty of enthusiasm for destroying cities anyway.

At the Potsdam Conference at the end of July, where the victorious Allies of Europe met, Truman hinted to STALIN he might have something up his sleeve. STALIN knew already but didn't let on in his trademark inscrutable paranoid warlord way. The Conference ended with a declaration warning Japan of 'prompt and utter destruction'.

The scene was set for 'the world to change for ever' as they might say going to a break on the History Channel. And then again when you came back from the adverts in case you'd forgotten what was happening in the programme you were watching.*

Hiroshima and then Nagasaki were bombed on the 6th and 9th of August, with the innocuously named bombs – Little Boy

---

* And tell you what, if and when this book ends up on the History Channel, which I love with all my heart by the way, that's how we're going to do it.

and Fat Man – Both cities were destroyed. More than 100,000 people were killed, including, in British news-programme style, 'one Briton'.

The Japanese government decided that, as the emperor – who was nothing to do with the war no sir not me – had said in his broadcast, 'the war situation has developed not necessarily to Japan's advantage', the cheeky, brazen bastard, and it threw in the bloodied towel.

Aftermath

Rather than make Germany sign another treaty, it was decided instead to cut the place in two: the Western Allies (including France) would control the west of Germany, and the Soviet Union the east – including Berlin.

And to make sure there were no more pesky disagreements about Germans living in places that weren't in Germany, millions of people were displaced from East Prussia and moved to Germany – simply kicked out. Poles were moved from the east of Poland into what had been Germany: STALIN saw this as a solution to making his borders safer, and at the time no one seemed to think it something worth making a fuss about. The war was over.

Europe buried its dead. Japan did the same. China sank into Revolutionary civil war. And the former Allies wondered 'what do we do now?' Ah yes, the COLD WAR. Though first, there was a bit of empire-crumbling to oversee.

PART 2:

POST – 1945

THE PARTITION OF INDIA, 1947:
LOOKS LIKE A SOLUTION

After the war ended, the British were immediately faced with their empire falling apart. The Attlee government – The-Greatest-Government-There-Ever-Was™ – was busy establishing the National Health Service and the welfare state and nationalising stuff and doing things specifically aimed at annoying Margaret Hilda Roberts who would later become TheThatcher.

The last thing the Attlee government – The-Greatest-Government-There-Ever-Was™ – wanted was to have to get bogged down in India when it had hiring nurses, train drivers, etc. to be getting on with.

Imperialism was over.* It was time to wind down the Raj. With sensitivity and respect.

---

* Imperialism.

Factors

- **Mahatma Gandhi:** In the Indian-Hindu corner you have Gandhi, who for decades had been infuriating the British by demanding independence but then not fighting for it. Nor wearing a suit and tie even though he was a lawyer.

→ Discuss: Which is more annoying: someone who refuses to do the simple thing and punch you in the face or someone who ignores the dress code?

- **Muhammad Ali Jinnah:** Very much in a suit and tie, super-smooth Muslim population rep Jinnah didn't seem averse to the idea of punching you in the face.

- **Jawaharlal Nehru:** Performing a super-smooth balancing act was Gandhi's successor Nehru, in line to be whatever India-was-to-be's first prime minister. Although the successor to the non-violent Gandhi, Nehru definitely seemed tasty, and he might well have sex with your wife.

→ Discuss: Choose your (non) fighter!

The Attlee government – The-Greatest-Government-There-Ever-Was™ – sent Lord Louis Mountbatten, long-limbed uber-smoothie and Royal family fixer, to India as viceroy to oversee independence.

Mountbatten lived like a man in a hurry, why, in 1942 he'd invaded France a whole two years early at Dieppe. Faced with the hugely complex problem of a continent's worth of people, races, princes, maharajahs, politicians and traditions, mixed together like a great big rich cake, he did what anyone would do with a cake and cut it in two. And buggered off. But only once Nehru had had sex with his wife. Probably. This left:

1. India – all the bits of India but not the bits with Muslims living in, roughly.
2. Pakistan – all the bits left mainly filled with Muslims, apart from the people living there who weren't Muslims. Roughly.

After all, in Ireland, partition – splitting the country into two chunks based mainly on religion – had worked out brilliantly.

Now, you wouldn't want to rush a thing like that, especially not in a country you had filled with trained soldiers and rifles, no sir, no ma'am.

India and Pakistan were born on 15 August 1947. CONGRATULATIONS, EVERYONE! IT'S A COUNTRY!

The only problem was that 14 million or so people were on the wrong side of the border that had been drawn up the month before. It happens.

Religious minorities were meant to stay put. After all, pre-Partition wasn't simply broken down into Muslims and non-Muslims: no, that would be too easy.

The British figure is that 200,000 people died in the upheaval that came with Partition – families trying to get to whichever country they felt they could live in, others being turfed out. Maybe the idea was to make India and Pakistan's formation such a traumatic process so as to make people come and live in the UK. Other estimates are that 1 million people lost their lives in the violence.

But back in Britain, as long as the Attlee government – The-Greatest-Government-There-Ever-Was™ – was shot of India and could get on with creating British Rail, then the less said about Partition the better.

And as if to demonstrate the **LESSON FROM HISTORY** that no good deed goes unpunished, Gandhi was assassinated for his trouble the year after Independence. Well done everyone.

MEANWHILE:

In the Middle East: as part of the post-colonial fallout of WERWERTWO Israel comes into existence and it is Israel, rather than, say, for example, the gigantic simultaneous calamity of Partition and the ongoing massive tensions over disputed territory, that that bloke who corners you in the pub and stands slightly too close to you with crisps in his beard bangs on about with his theories about who runs the world, and well what would the reason for that be, eh?

THE COLD WAR

The Cold War was a period of human History where for the first time in its History humanity had at its disposal the means to destroy the planet, and for a vast chunk of that period, seemed quite into the idea. If only to stop the other guy destroying the planet.

The reason? Well – that's pretty simple. WERWERTWO ended with the Nazis suitably vanquished and ready to become the main attraction of GCSE History. The Japanese surrendered as a result of having it emphatically underlined how they'd lost the war at Hiroshima and Nagasaki. You'd think, therefore, what with the tens of millions dead, the vast, almost imponderable cost and the mountain range of reconstruction that was subsequently needed, that the idea of any more war might have been unlikely.

Post-war cooperation between the Allies extended to the Nuremberg Trials, where top and middling Nazis were put on trial and crimes against humanity were debated cagily by all participants, none of whose hands were necessarily clean. These trials kept the hangman busy, but the business of what to do about Europe, and in particular Germany, remained. The USA adopted the Marshall Plan – pumping millions of dollars into the European economy for rebuilding and renewal. The Soviets established governments sympathetic to the UUSSRRRRR in the way that Kermit the Frog was sympathetic to Jim Henson. As the reason for the two very different superpowers (they were called that now) to stick together receded into the past, their differences of approach and understanding of how the new world would work out came to the fore.

In other words:

- CAPITALISM VERSUS COMMUNISM;
- LIBERTY VERSUS SLAVERY;
- THE ANTI-COLONIAL AMERICAN EMPIRE VERSUS THE ANTI-IMPERIAL RUSSIAN EMPIRE;
- RUNNING DOGS OF IMPERIALIST YANKEE LACKEY STATES VERSUS NOBLE WORKERS OF THE WORLD.

You know, I never have had the stomach for all the slogans.

There were three huge, gigantic and – to use a word that gets wheeled out in these situations – seismicolitical side-Effects of the war.

1. It showed war worked if you did it properly. Unlike DOUBLEYOUDOUBLEYOU ONE, WERWERTWO ended with a conclusive result that the losing parties, no matter how hard they tried, couldn't dispute.

2. The war had elevated the USA and the USSSRRR from non-interested distant isolated cousin and self-throttling paranoid backwater respectively, into colossal, unprecedented superpowers, with tons of weapons and no one to fire them at. They had got to this state and got what they wanted by the application of (1).

3. ALSO! The way they had managed to make war such a success for them both was by being either *very* capitalist[*] or *very* Soviet[†] and both were brimming with confidence in the way they did things and bristling with weaponry that embodied that confidence.

Two political systems, philosophically not to the other's taste, energised by militarisation – what could possibly go wrong?

(Bear in mind there were a couple of years after WERWERTWO when it looked like the USA and USSRRR were going to get along just fine, but in the end a six of American politics' rampant bonkers paranoia, and a half a dozen of STALIN's rampant bonkers paranoia got the better of everyone. This two-year friendly hiatus Causes considerable anxiety with hindsight that all the actual anxiety at the time could have been avoided had the USA and the USSRRRR just been able to get past the fact they were better off as allies, even though there wasn't a prawn cocktail's chance on a buffet of that ever being possible.)

---

* While at the same time ditching basic capitalist stuff by basically the government paying for everything in, erm, a communist style.

† By, erm, ditching a load of Soviet stuff by being super-patriotic about Russia.

The Cold War had everything! The threat of nuclear annihilation! Massive arms build-ups! Paranoia! And showbiz!

Paranoia!

The USA slid into anti-communist paranoia, helped enormously by communists spying on America and passing nuclear secrets to the Soviets. The kind of thing that might well make you paranoid.

This paranoia had a cheerleader in the form of Senator Robert McCarthy. McCarthy is one of those people whose name gets wheeled out as an insult, and fair enough. He was a blinkered, opportunistic, ambitious bastard, who took the inch offered to him by the Soviet spies that had been uncovered in the US defence establishment and ran a marathon. McCarthy ramped up the fear of reds under the bed. There were communists everywhere! Undermining America! And being, of all things, Un-American!

Showbiz!

Now of course this wouldn't normally be something we'd concern ourselves with in a History book written this side of what dribblers call The Pond, but fortunately for your and my attention span McCarthy's activities led to the involvement of Hollywood. The House Committee on Un-American Activities sought to find out who the Reds under Hollywood's beds were, and major stars were accused.

The problem was lots of stars had, during the war at least, been enthusiastic fans of the USSRRRR, what with it being the USA's ally in the struggle to defeat Nazism, something it was agreed was a GOOD THING.

Some had even made propaganda films about the Soviets at the behest of the US government, the filthy traitors. Others had been interested in COMMUNISM because, well, they found it inter-esting. Land of the free, innit? as someone might say in a manner drenched in bitter irony. Big stars such as Charlie Chaplin and Orson Welles refused to testify to the committee, regarding it as a show trial of people's political conscience, a.k.a. Un-American. The Hollywood studios, panicked by the idea of appearing to be pro-Commie,* blacklisted hundreds of writers, actors and others.

Because this happened in English and to glamorous people, some of the nitty gritty of actual alleged communists and Soviet spies in the American defence establishment and elsewhere gets forgotten. Characters such as Alger Hiss, who may or may not have been a Soviet spy, for instance, but Alger Hiss never made any movies so it's hard to get anyone to care.

As the Fifties progressed, the Americans armed like mad in response to the thought that the Soviets might be arming, which they were. Everything was about the Cold War; the Cold War was about everything. And not just between the two main (non) combatants. Everyone else got caught up in it too, whether they liked it or not.

Peace for all mankind: the Cold War in the rest of the world

The Cold War of course never came to any fighting: at no point did the forces of Communism and anti-Communism come to blows, that's the main thing. Except in China. And

---

* To adopt the vernacular.

Korea. And Greece. And Paraguay. And Malaya, ooh yeah that was bad. And Algeria. And Sudan – can't leave Sudan off the list. And Tibet. And Vietnam. And Angola. And depending on how you look at it, Israel, Egypt, Syria, Jordan. And Namibia. And Congo. Eritrea! Aden too. Iran. Iraq. Lebanon. Nigeria – everyone got mixed up in that. Laos. Cambodia, yes definitely. Mozambique. Afghanistan in the Eighties. And the rest. And Chile and Argentina and Peru. And Nicaragua. Other than all that fighting, all over the world, no fighting.

People in countries eager to exit whichever European empire they were part of could expect help from the Soviets or from the Americans. The Soviets exported their most successful Revolutionary product, the AK-47 Kalashnikov assault rifle – cheap and cheerful and responsible for far more deaths than any atomic bomb. The Americans dished out M16s, or when they wanted it to look like they weren't involved, Kalashnikovs. Coup and countercoup saw one grim ruling elite replaced by another, backed by one side or the other, like a tag wrestling match that actually mattered for once. Power was what mattered. And no fighting of course. It was a Cold War, you see.

The Cold War became the backdrop to the rest of the Twentieth Century up until 1990: though you'd have to ask someone from Vietnam what it was like to be on the receiving end of this backdrop. When it did end, everything that had been ravelled unravelled. But we'll get to that.

THE SUEZ CRISIS:
LOCATION LOCATION LOCATION

The Suez Crisis (1956, but honestly, don't worry about the dates) usually comes up in the form of the sentence 'worst crisis since Suez' or 'national humiliation on a par with Suez' or just 'like Suez?'

This means you don't need to know what happened, and you're saved the bother of remembering where it happened because it comes handily labelled. It happened in Suez. But what happened? Apart from a terrible crisis and national humiliation the likes of which has happened a lot since, etc. etc.

It pays to be informed so here we go, back to the period when the British and French knew that their time as mighty empires was over, and it was time to withdraw and redraw the world map, reduce colonial commitments and so on, and therefore decided to invade Egypt.*

---

* Imperialism, innit.

Causes

- In the nineteenth century, the British and French built the Suez Canal.
- At the time, canals and railways were the way powerful Western countries liked to show they were there to help rather than simply help themselves to stuff.
- Very often the canal or the railway's job was to move the stuff from say, Suez, back to London or Paris or even Brussels.

The Suez Canal very simply provides a connection between the Red Sea and the Mediterranean, saving you the long sea journey around Africa – essential in the British Empire in India and further east for getting goods to Blighty quicker. Of course, in the time of easyJet to Magaluf for a pound – and those days will return, believe me – this probably doesn't seem that big a deal.

When completed in 1869, the canal, built by Ferdinand de Lesseps* – at twice the original builder's estimate – made world trade quicker and more efficient than ever. Going over budget also meant that the Egyptians involved in building it went bust, so to help them out the British invaded Egypt to make sure the

---

* There's your pub quiz fact.

canal remained in safe hands. As you do. Nice canal you've got here, shame if something were to happen to it.

- In 1956, the British Empire was basically bankrupt as a result of winning WERWERTWO and faced lots of decisions about how exactly to cope with being broke and sorting out the colonies and countries that wanted out of the empire.
- Americans were really busy worrying about how best to nuke–avoid being nuked by the Soviet Union.
- The UK had got out of Egypt but, along with the French government, held onto the Suez Canal, on the grounds that they'd paid for it and anyway it wasn't like Egypt would want it for shipping things through, what with the canal already being in Egypt.
- The Egyptians had a change of government, from King Farouk to a military man, Colonel Abdel Nasser. Nasser was a pan-Arabist – he believed all the Arabs in the world should unite and work together for a better Arab future with one Arab in charge who would show the way. No prizes for guessing who.
- Because the Suez Canal was in Egypt, he decided that it should belong to Egypt. Controversial.

The British and French governments weren't having it. The British prime minister Anthony Eden, who had spent something like fifteen years waiting for Churchill to retire and/or die – something Churchill seemed about to do every other year – was finally in charge and wasn't prepared to see Nasser take over the canal. The French agreed. Eden went to see Nasser in Cairo and even though Eden could speak Arabic, he insisted on speaking English and lecturing Nasser about how he should know his place. This went down about as well as you might expect. Eden went home and painted a picture of Nasser as a future HITLER who couldn't be appeased. The French agreed.

Dirty weekend

The British and the French decided that they were going to have to seize the Suez Canal. Israel got involved, keen on getting one over Nasser, who had made all sorts of threatening noises about wiping Israel off the face of the earth.

The British and the French and the Israelis had all got together and getting together was something that had to be denied. To make it properly seedy and dirty-weekend-French they'd met in a hotel in a Parisian suburb.

The Special Relationship

The Americans weren't happy about all this. US president Ike Eisenhower wasn't happy with the UK doing whatever it liked, especially as he had been trying to get Nasser onside. Also – as with lots of History – there's a MEANWHILE.

The MEANWHILE was that Hungary had had enough of being a Soviet satellite state. The UUUUSR, on the other hand, hadn't. Soviet tanks had rolled into the Hungarian capital Budapest on 4 November 1956 – the day before the British and French landed in Egypt – and put down the uprising. The COLD WAR meant the USA's priority wasn't its old Allies; instead it was trying to make sure things didn't kick off with the Soviets. Eisenhower told the British and the French to knock it off and threatened to collapse the pound. Sod the Special Relationship.

Consequences

Eden had to resign: he had lied to the House of Commons about what had happened, and whether the whole thing had been planned in advance. This mattered more than the fact the whole thing had been a total cock-up. He was sick at the time; he'd had operations on his gall bladder and had been at the medicine cabinet.

The UK was exposed as a not-so-superpower, Suez was the

Worst Crisis Ever, soon to become the gold standard of British political humiliation, against which all foreign policy disasters would be judged.

The French decided the best idea for them was to set up some kind of European cooperation thing, the British decided that probably wasn't for them, but also decided it might be time to get out of the empire business, leaving Cyprus and Aden and most of the African countries in which it had a toe-hold in something of a rush, claiming that a 'wind of change' was blowing rather than simply admitting time was up. The Americans went on to say that the British had lost an empire but never found a role, which makes them sound like a senile person at a buffet.

Imperial exit, bloodshed, rebellion, disaster and national awakening followed.*

LESSON FROM HISTORY

Invade the Middle East if you like, just don't lie about it.

---

* Imperialism. This one's a doozy: even when you stop doing Imperialism, that's bad too.

THE INVENTION OF SEX

It goes without saying that the Twentieth Century is well known as the first century that anyone had SEX. In future centuries this will be the thing that the years 1900–2000 or thereabouts will be remembered for, above all else.

The History of SEX is as follows:

- While the ancients theorised about SEX and the Romans wrote about what they reckoned it might be like, religion did what it could to discourage any such activity.
- Depictions of what was considered to be SEX are few and far between throughout the History of art. Even though from the Renaissance onwards paintings of nude people were not uncommon, the very last thing any of them were doing in those paintings was having SEX.
- Such a paucity of evidence for SEX leaves this historian to conclude that – apart from the occasional freakish and immediately regretted outbreak – **there was no SEX until the mid- to late Twentieth Century.**

Certainly, the Victorians seemed so horrified by SEX there can be no way they ever had any: Victorian writing about SEX makes it fairly clear to the disinterested reader that they didn't have much idea what it was like. In general they made it clear what a bad idea they thought it was, and even wore clothes designed to make sure it was unlikely ever to cross anyone's mind and deeply impractical to attempt. Ask anyone actually wearing a corset; you can barely breathe in those things, let alone engage in vigorous activity of any kind. So, there is some consolation in the thought that while the Twentieth Century is unarguably a time of unprecedented horrors, some of these horrors are maybe counterbalanced by the fact that cuddles finally became special.

At the start of the century, talk of SEX was mainly confined to literary salons and books theorising about who would be allowed to have SEX and under what circumstances. Conclusions were that on balance no one should be having SEX, least of all men with other men, and that women couldn't possibly enjoy it. Before DOUBLEYOUDOUBLEYOU ONE, the psychologist Sigmund Freud had suggested that all anyone really wanted deep down was to have SEX; public opinion agreed that what he was saying seemed a bit far-fetched and that he probably had a dirty mind. The war interrupted this talk of coitus, and so the debate of whether SEX was something anyone would want to do, let alone like, was put on hold for four years.

The Twenties and Thirties

During the ROARING TWENTIES there were suggestions that people might be thinking about having SEX. Fashions reached a point where clothes were a) flattering to the figure and likely to result in admiration and/or fancying someone and b) easier to take off. At the same time, women in the Western world found themselves wearing trousers, which caused confusion for some men planning to have SEX with them, or something.

So, SEX was clearly on the agenda in the Twenties, and the Thirties was fraught with sexual tension – to the point of King Edward VIII giving up being king because he'd made it quite clear he was interested in having SEX with an American woman, easily the most scandalous thought a monarch had ever had, so little wonder it cost him his throne (see ABDICATION CRISIS).

Happily, before any actual SEX could occur, WERWERTWO intervened and everyone spent the next six years trying to kill each other instead, which you have to agree was a lucky escape.

The Fifties

The Fifties saw the idea of having SEX back on the agenda – helped along by the likes of Elvis Presley who made it quite clear how up for it he was, gyrating and rubbing himself on the microphone stand like a dog with a cushion. Presley was building on the work done by the likes of Frank Sinatra who had certainly been suggestive about the idea of SEX without rubbing himself on anything, instead relying on admiring glances and smart remarks. It is fair to say that had it not been for pioneers like Elvis Presley it seems unlikely that SEX would have broken out before the 1970s or 1980s or maybe even later.

The Sixties: everyone's at it

Nevertheless, come the 1960s – so to speak – and SEX broke out all over the world. Even the poet Philip Larkin, a man you'd think was as unlikely to be interested in SEX as any, wrote about it. In the wake of the likes of Elvis, you had the likes of The Beatles and The Rolling Stones, who made it entirely clear that yes, they had had SEX, and indeed it was great fun and everyone really ought to try it too.

This sexual Revolution had polite society aghast, even as they tried it for themselves. Immediately, scientists got working on a cure, and aside from the condom, which as anyone will tell you is terribly off-putting at best, soon invented the Pill, designed to make sure women weren't going to have SEX ever again, by making it too embarrassing to have to ask a doctor for a prescription. Unfortunately, one of the side Effects of the Pill was it made sure you couldn't get pregnant and the rest is History, which is why it's in this book.

As the Sixties unrolled into the Seventies and SEX took hold of everyone, so it seemed, everyone wanted to get in on it, including men who wanted to have SEX with men – previously regarded as totally unlikely – women who wanted to have SEX with other women – again, who could possibly have imagined something like that – and all the other variants of this fun and exciting activity there are under the sun.

This new attitude to SEX, called by some the permissive society, led to all sorts of legal reforms, including the decriminalisation of SEX between men over the age of twenty-one in 1967. It wasn't just that criminalisation was unfair, it hadn't exactly stopped anyone anyway.

By the time the Eighties came along, the novelty had worn off for a lot of people, especially as it turned out there were diseases that could be transmitted by SEX. The Eighties saw a particularly deadly new disease make its appearance: HIV and AIDS. Because people were still getting used to the idea that anyone was having SEX, let alone men with other men, it took a great deal to get the powers-that-were to take HIV and AIDS seriously. While lots of effective drugs have been developed to deal with HIV, what it meant was that SEX was something everyone had to talk about and consequently, ended up doing.

The outbreak of SEX in the Sixties has been blamed for pretty much everything: families breaking down, society crumbling, culture getting debased and so on, teenagers, loud music, late trains, traffic jams, pancakes sticking to the ceiling, fizzy water not being as fizzy as it used to be, flooding, too much sunshine, earthquakes, bad telly and worse films, and generally spreading new kinds of deeper human misery. Given the thousands of years of human History that preceded SEX breaking out I'd say that's quite a claim.

SEX on the page: the *Lady Chatterley's Lover* trial

At the cutting edge of the SEX explosion was the novel *Lady Chatterley's Lover* by self-styled dour and troubled author D. H. Lawrence. *Lady Chatterley's Lover* contained what were seen as needlessly graphic – pornographic even – descriptions of SEX. Lawrence had tried to have the book published in 1928 but it was deemed too controversial and so he had to publish it himself. Penguin decided to publish the book in 1960, and was immediately prosecuted for obscenity.

If you haven't read it – and if you're expecting pictures because it's a saucy book you're going to be disappointed – it's the story of a woman whose marriage drifts into alienation who has an affair with the gamekeeper on her husband's estate. Lord Chatterley has been injured in DOUBLEYOUDOUBLEYOU ONE and can't satisfy Lady Chatterley. The gamekeeper is happy to oblige. Apart from him being a gamekeeper and not a plumber it's as standard a porn video plot as you could hope to meet. In book form.

The trial caused a sensation. The prosecution misjudged the mood by asking the jury a simple enough question that set the

tone for the rest of the proceedings: 'Would you approve of your young sons, young daughters – because girls can read as well as boys – reading this book? Is it a book you would have lying around your own house? Is it a book that you would even wish your wife or your servants to read?' And by the end of it – via thirty-five defence witnesses including politicians, literary experts and the Bishop of Woolwich – Penguin won the case and the book was published, just in time to coincide with the outbreak of SEX across the world.

SEX goes political: The Profumo affair, 1963

The Profumo affair is one of the great scandals in British political History, marking the first time anyone in political circles in Britain had had SEX. SEX (see SEX) had only just broken out and politicians like everyone else were keen to find out what all the fuss was about.

Before we get into the whole imbroglio*, the thing to remember about the Profumo affair is that for a really long time, it was as though it was the only scandal that had ever happened in British politics. Just like SUEZ, Profumo became the thing everything else got compared to, almost as if no one was paying attention to anything else that happened since. Profumo did resign though, which may come as a shock to some readers.

---

* If ever you see that word in a book it means the author has won a bet.

Here are the eight key Profumo facts which make it the **greatest scandal of all time**:

1. Naked swimming pool parties!
2. Pesky Russians!
3. The possibility of SEX having happened!
4. Beautiful women photographed in chairs provocatively!
5. The establishment closes ranks!
6. A cooked-up court case!
7. Lying to Parliament is bad!
8. John Profumo resigning in disgrace, his political career over, stepping back from public life, rather than hanging on pointlessly and further damaging the Macmillan government, and devoting the rest of his life to charity working in the East End of London as a volunteer and fundraiser, eventually finding his way back to a lower-profile kind of respectability most likely as a way of making amends for where he'd gone wrong.

John Profumo, dyed-in-the-wool Tory, super-posh, handsome, married-to-a-film-star smoothie type, was the Secretary of State for War in the Macmillan government. There being no war on – the CUBAN MISSILE CRISIS had occurred only the year before and had for the moment really put people off the idea of war – he had plenty of time on his hands. He spent that time indulging in the exciting new pastime of SEX, and went to parties where SEX would occur, or at least be on the agenda.

These parties were organised by an osteopath called Stephen Ward, who knew lots of people who were also into the new SEX craze and was there in case they put their backs out.

As well as women who were, astonishingly, interested in having SEX – including the teenage models/showgirls Mandy Rice-Davies and Christine Keeler – the Russian naval attaché Yevgeny Ivanov* attended the same parties, presumably reporting back to the USSRRRRR on the fascinating new activity sweeping the UK. This was the business end of the SEX scandal, so to speak. The women got the blame, of course.

Profumo had to quit as secretary of state for war, not because he had failed to start and win a war, but because he had lied to Parliament. Lying to Parliament is of course much, much worse than the possible security breach involved in sleeping with someone who was also sleeping with a Russian Intelligence officer at the height of the COLD WAR. Standards.

---

* It's not an anagram of spy but it should be.

THE CULTURAL REVOLUTION: HOLY MAO!

MEANWHILE in China: after WERWERTWO there had been a civil war that ended with the Communist Party under Chairman Mao in charge. Mao immediately got cracking with turning China into a Workers' Paradise, mainly by finding everyone work to do: he got industry started in China and set about explaining how the party was now the supreme authority in China and things were going to be different round here from now on etc.

Mao had fought a long and canny war, and wasn't going to let anyone get in his way now he was in charge. This meant ~~oppression, famine, wars in Korea and Vietnam and a big falling-out with Taiwan you can't even talk about as well as~~ China's economy was growing rapidly and its population with it, ~~despite the huge famine during the Cultural Revolution in the Sixties caused by, amongst other hare-brained stuff, the Mao government insisting everyone hand in their woks to be made into steel and the abject failure of collective farming, which~~

killed millions. Nevertheless it meant that by the end of the
Sixties China was recognised as a world player in the East.

In terms of culture, the party made sure that people were
kept ruthlessly on message with Mao's *Little Red Book*, a
compendium of political theory, known as Maoism (Mao had

named the theory after himself, always a winner), that stoked people up in relentlessly paranoid style against confected enemies of the Revolution, such as teachers, lawyers, even people who worked for the government, turning China into a bearpit of denunciation and personal treachery, requiring considerable mental gymnastics while the Communist Party top brass carried on like some sort of hideous soap opera.

China kept itself to itself politically, apart from sending soldiers to fight in Korea and helping the Vietnamese, though six of one, half a dozen of the other, you might say, and when Chairman Mao died in 1976 everyone in China, though let's be honest it's impossible to say what anyone thought, knew that whatever was round the corner could hardly be worse than him.

Come the 1980s the Chinese government had shaken off the worst excesses of Mao's time in office but found the balancing act of relaxing oppression and yet retaining total control really difficult and even contradictory, as greater freedoms were established so they threatened the party's dominance. Were the reforms cosmetic or meaningful? This tension in the end led to the notorious Tiananmen Square Massacre, an uprising that was brutally crushed in a way that looked as though it might undermine the legitimacy of the Chinese Communist Party. The lone man who stood in front of the tanks in 1989 represented the repression that the government stood for and its willingness to oppress the population.

How about we cheer ourselves up with the story of how the world wasn't destroyed in a nuclear inferno?

THE CUBAN MISSILE CRISIS, 1962

The COLD WAR reached its height – and its riskiest moment – in 1962 with the Cuban Missile Crisis.

CUBAN MISSILE CRISIS SHORT VERSION: NOTHING HAPPENED.

Explaining that nothing happened is simple enough; explaining *why* nothing happened takes some doing.

Khrushchev: nicer than the other guy

In short, with the Death of STALIN (Netflix, from Friday 14th) the Soviet Union underwent a process of readjustment and refinement, and once STALIN was good and cold – people were really, really scared of him even when he was dead – Nikita Khrushchev elbowed his way to the front of the Communist Party in 1953 and became First Secretary. This involved more than taking dictation and opening the mail.

Khrushchev decided that what needed to happen in the USSSSR, though gradually, was a move away from Stalinism, putting domestic reform at the centre of his programme and generally being nicer than his predecessor. He even had a cheeky nickname: Niki.

Khrushchev had of course been up to his neck in it during the STALIN era; he wouldn't have survived otherwise, let alone made it to the top as a party apparatchik. You could argue that aiming to be nicer than STALIN is a pretty low bar but props nevertheless, Niki. He did what he could to reset, nay modernise, the Soviet Union:

- Denouncing STALIN with a speech in 1956 to party delegates, which was kept secret but then leaked – this pretty much epitomises how he was loosening things up.
- He built great big blocks of flats.
- He tried to fix farming which had been entirely scrambled and screwed by STALIN.
- He tried to move Soviet technology and industry along from some of the pre-war practices that STALIN had in place. Including the forced work kind of industry, like the Gulag.
- To find the money to do this stuff, he shifted military spending away from conventional forces (tanks: lots and lots of tanks) towards nuclear rockets. Because nukes, expensive as they are, are cheaper than loads of

soldiers standing around picking their noses waiting for
something to happen.

- PLUS! He helped out with other countries that leaned
  towards COMMUNISM wherever they were in the
  world, maintaining the Soviet policy of pissing off the
  US any which way it could. Again this was cheaper
  than loads and loads of Russian squaddies sitting around
  in East Germany wondering what the point was.

As the Fifties drew to a close, the consequences of Khrushchev's reforms and the US's response to them assumed their
own momentum.

MEANWHILE in the USA

JFK had become the Youngest-President-Ever in 1960 and,
although he was a Democrat and had made it clear he was nothing
like his Republican predecessor Eisenhower, Kennedy set about
being Iker than Ike when it came to dealing with the USSSR.

One of the things JFK had decided to get tough on was Cuba.
As far as the USA was concerned, Cuba was an offshore Miami
more Miami than Miami. Cubans weren't so sure, however, and
a Revolution brewed for most of the Fifties, ending up with
the delightful* Fidel Castro in charge.

---

* **Depending on who you ask.**

The USA was kicked out of Cuba, apart from the great big military base in Guantanamo Bay, which Castro decided was probably best left as it was, rather than directly taking on the Americans. Initially a free-range, good-time, president-for-life, brother-as-deputy Revolutionary, Castro made friends with the USSSSR and by the time JFK had become the Youngest-President-Ever he was very cosy with Khrushchev.

JFK had made all sorts of promises about what he'd do about Cuba. The CIA, hiring miffed Cuban exiles, tried to invade at the Bay of Pigs in 1961. Were it not so serious, it would be hilarious, but it turned out that planeloads of plantation owners and other assorted annoyed rich people maybe weren't the best people to send in to overthrow Castro.

But what about the missiles? This is a missile crisis, right?

Khrushchev regarded Cuba as too good a trolling opportunity to miss, and proposed sending short-range nuclear weapons to Cuba, along with plenty of 'advisers'. Castro, wanting to make sure the US didn't invade again, was understandably keen. The USSSSSR argued that the USA had stationed Jupiter nuclear missiles in Turkey on its border as part of its NATO commitment, so how was Cuba any different? So in the summer of 1962, the Soviets started sending men and weapons to Cuba. JFK, who'd staked his political reputation as the Youngest-President-Ever on being tough on commies, had little option but to be unhappy about the missile deployments. Well, Cuba is only 90 miles from Florida.

SO: the actual Cuban Missile Crisis, October 1962 – what you need to know about how we nearly fried

Khrushchev's missile facilities were spotted by a U-2 spy plane flying over Cuba in the summer. The White House argued about what to do next. The options, according to Vice President Lyndon B. Johnson were:

1. Do nothing: American vulnerability to Soviet missiles was not new. Involves the least bother. Let it lie. Get used to it. Get over it. Move on. Why make a fuss?
2. Diplomacy: Use diplomatic pressure to get the Soviet Union to remove the missiles. Might/might not work – the Soviets were on a roll; had they not demonstrated what cool tech they had by sending a metal football around the world with a beeper in it?
3. Secret approach: Offer Castro the choice of splitting with the Russians or being invaded. As if he'd keep that to himself.
4. Invasion, air strikes, blockade. The idea being that would calm things down.

At a glance my money would have been on doing nothing. Now, get this, and please don't be amazed, the US joint chiefs of staff – the people in charge of the army, navy and air force – recommended invading Cuba. JFK didn't agree. He was worried that an invasion would provoke the Soviets to take Berlin in retaliation.* A classic MEANWHILE.

Although the idea of missiles just down the road might have been freaking out the military top brass, people close to JFK weren't so sure. Defense† Secretary Robert McNamara regarded Option 1 as the only sensible way of looking at it. Do nothing. And, frankly he may have been right. The complication was that there were elections in 1962. Mid-term, JFK didn't want to give the impression that he wasn't tough on COMMUNISM, or weak on Cuba and Castro. Which meant he knew that Option 1 wouldn't work politically, even if it was by far the most sensible, actually. What does that tell you? That sometimes people won't do nothing even when nothing is the right thing to do. Ah don't worry about it, it's a long time ago.

Diplomacy! That'll fix it! JFK meets the Soviet foreign minister Gromyko and they get into a row, or at least half a row about the missile placements, Kennedy not letting Gromyko know what he knew on the grounds that letting the Russians know what he knew would show he knew more than they thought he knew though they knew perfectly well he knew. You know. And as it was, he didn't know that much so all he really let them know was that he didn't really know.

So, while the US air force flew over Cuba in a generally

---

* It's worth remembering that when stuff was happening in Berlin, he'd be worrying about what would happen in Cuba.

† And remember this is Dee-fence as in Off-ence.

threatening manner – you know the sort of thing, 'Please shoot at us and then we can shoot at you oops oh no did we invade?' – JFK made up his mind about what to do next, as the main cargo of the USSSSR's missiles was on its way to Cuba. (What the US didn't know was the Soviets had already got nuclear weapons to Cuba, including some pilotless jet planes with atom bombs in them pointed at Guantanamo Bay. Phew. Luckily they knew nothing about them.)

In the end, the USA settled on Option 4, the naval blockade. Strictly speaking, a blockade is an act of war, though the Americans called it a quarantine, saying they'd stop vessels to check for military equipment. And what do you know? Up went the tension. On 22 October, the blockade began.

'The rest of the world watched and held its breath'*

On the 25th, the Americans went to what they called DEFCON 2. This was one down from going to war – it meant that American bombers, B-52s and B-47s, loaded up with nuclear bombs, were on permanent patrol over the Arctic Circle, making pouncing on Russia and nuking it dead easy. The rest of the world went purple and started gurning.

On the 27th, a U-2 spy plane over Cuba was shot down. More tension. This wasn't helped by the US navy dropping 'warning'

---

* I've made this quote up but boy it fits.

grenades in the direction of a Soviet sub they had detected. The Russian sub, the snappily named *B-59*, was armed with nuclear torpedoes and the crew then debated whether to fire back with its nukes – which would have escalated the situation somewhat. The captain wanted to launch his nukes, but he needed the nod from three officers on board. One of them, Vasily Arkhipov, said no, best not, and so the Third World War didn't break out that Saturday.

You haven't heard of him, yet he probably saved the world, and he did it by doing nothing.

At the same time, an American U-2 spy plane somehow

found itself over the USSSSSSR and the Soviets scrambled jets to shoot it down. The Americans responded with their own planes. Planes armed with nuclear anti-aircraft missiles. Argh. Because nuclear anti-aircraft missiles are a thing.

Endgame?

All this tension led to JFK and Khrushchev – he was a secretary remember? he couldn't help himself – writing each

other some pretty stern letters, I can tell you, each telling the other off. Both of them were being egged on by the people around them – JFK was being urged to get tough on Cuba and the Soviets, Castro was in Khrushchev's ear demanding war with the Americans. Finally, Khrushchev wrote to Kennedy and suggested that the US remove its Jupiter nuclear missiles from Turkey. Khrushchev might have been an idiot getting himself into this situation, but he was no fool getting out of it – he made his offer to disarm Cuba in a letter (again) that the whole world could read. Kennedy resisted the pressure from his own military to start World War Three and jumped at the chance.

But because he might have been an idiot to get into this situation, JFK was no fool getting out of it either, and he didn't make public that the Jupiters would be removed from Turkey. That way, Kennedy ended up looking like he had defeated Khrushchev over Cuba, and squashed Castro's plans of being a colossal pain in America's backside.

Consequences: it's an ill wind

Aside from not blowing the world up and resulting in the deaths of everyone on Cuba, hundreds of millions of American and Soviet citizens as well as everyone in between, the Cuban Missile Crisis resulted in the telephone hotline between Washington and Moscow being set up.

If this was the beginning of the end for the letter, oh well never mind.

And now that bit after the film
where they tell you what happened next

This is one of those events which seems to pan out back to front – nothing good came of doing nothing for the people who knew that doing nothing was the right thing to do:

JFK was murdered the following year (see THE ASSASSINATION OF JFK).

Khrushchev, who had averted the nuclear war he had almost wandered into, lost his job two years later because the USSSSSSSSSR being humiliated on the world stage was worse than the world stage being blasted to atoms.

And **Castro** stayed in power in Cuba until 2011, dying in 2016, despite Cuba being blockaded by the US during the COLD WAR, then after that despite Cuba being pretty much the only communist state left apart from North Korea. He spent that entire time doing the Cuban equivalent of flicking Vs at the US, something he would never have been able to do if the Americans had done what he wanted and nuked the place.

You can't please everyone, can you?

THE ASSASSINATION OF JFK, 1963

Lee Harvey Oswald. That's it. Honestly, if you want to waste your own and everyone else's time, by all means go online and figure out how it must have been the Mafia with the CIA and the Soviets using a Cuban middleman on the orders of Lyndon B. Johnson to set up the patsy with the magic bullet who was Oswald's double anyway. I'm sure you'll enjoy it. But seriously.

JFK* was killed by Lee Harvey Oswald in Dealey Plaza and that's all you need know. People determined to tell you otherwise, other than maybe Oswald's wife or his mum – who you'd expect to say that – are doing it because it makes them feel like they are in control of the event somehow. And that is not how History works. History is out of control, a runaway train with no stations, the occasional nice view and easy gradient, but with no timetable, none of the stops you'd like to

---

* Watch any documentary about JFK and be thrilled to learn that JFK was the youngest man to become president ever, possibly even ever to be born, and that he was – appropriately for the 1960s – the first US president ever to have SEX.

get off at, no buffet car, no drinks for when you're delayed, no sandwiches devised by TV chef James Martin, no return ticket, no rhyme, no reason. It is entirely pointless to try to impose one.

Kennedy's decisions, such as they were – to try to invade Cuba, bolster the US effort in the VIETNAM WAR and almost get everyone nuked in the CUBAN MISSILE CRISIS – do somewhat undermine anyone trying to tell you what a top geezer he was and how the world might have been a better place were it not for the marksmanship course Oswald had been on when he was a US Marine. However, any JFK balance sheet has to include Marilyn Monroe, one of the great pioneers of having SEX in the 1960s.

Let's talk about The Beatles, shall we?

BEATLEMANIA, 1963
AND ONWARDS FOR ALL TIME

Just like SEX, until the 1960s there was no entertainment. There were things that looked like 'hey, might be entertaining', things that people liked, but not *that* much. Anyone who tried to break the mould didn't: Elvis still had to go into the army and do the draft.

That was until 1963, when The Beatles took the world by storm with a world-shattering combo of moptop hair and shrill harmonies. Oh God, writing about music is *hard*.

Author's note:

Honestly, how anyone can write about The Beatles without modern readers knowing everything about them beats me. They're The Beatles, the Fab Four. You know the words to all of their songs even if you've never heard them. It's hardwired. They formed a band as kids called The Quarrymen, went to art school, went to Hamburg, learned their trade, listened to lots of American music, loved the Goons and music hall and soul music, got rejected by Decca, ditched the drummer, now they're John Paul George and Ringo, grew their hair, made movies, got screamed at wherever they went, bigger than Jesus, records burned, more screaming, were thrown out of the Philippines for annoying Imelda Marcos, played Shea Stadium, grew their hair some more, did drugs, had more hits, stopped touring, their music got smarter and more produced, George Martin, more drugs, *Sgt. Pepper*, more drugs, Brian Epstein died, they got a bit lost, Macca grew a big tache, *Magical Mystery Tour* movie flopped, Yoko Ono on the scene, less screaming more dreaming, *The White Album*, things start going awry, Ringo says he's had enough, leaves, comes back, they film making an album with lots of tension, play a concert on the roof at Apple in Savile Row, then John Paul George and Ringo look like they're going to break up and teeter for a bit on the brink and finally break up with their swansong *Abbey Road* recorded last but released penultimately and all of this happens in ONLY SEVEN YEARS. IT'S THE BIGGEST 'MEANWHILE' IN ALL HUMAN HISTORY.

Some facts about The Beatles:

- When it comes to entertainment, The Beatles are the difference between then and now.

- They catalysed everything, including themselves. (Now that's good: that's proper music writing.)
- Anyone who says they don't like them is doing it to impress you. It's not impressive.
- In the USSR, the Beatles were seen as a product of the corrupting capitalist industrial culture.
- In the USA, they were godless youth-corrupting communist propaganda.

CIVIL RIGHTS MOVEMENT:
FIGHT FOR YOUR RIGHT
TO HAVE RIGHTS

When WERWERTWO ended, everyone agreed all over the world that HITLER and Nazism had made racism look really bad. Even other racists thought so. Really bad. It was almost as if he had ruined racism for everyone.

Almost.

When Martin Luther King spoke at the Lincoln Memorial in 1963 and said 'I have a dream' he wasn't talking about the kind of dreams most of us have: running through a corridor with a thousand doors only to discover our legs are made of corduroy, having to sit in on drums for The Who while naked, and making sweet love with Mrs Arnold.

MLK's dream was essentially boring, mundane, ordinary. No climbing the Eiffel Tower to find a sky made of cake at the top for him.

His dream was about kids going to school. Sitting where they want on the bus. Being able to go into a shop and say 'hello' without being murdered. Voting. Being able to marry who you fall in love with. Having somewhere to live, etc. etc.

None of that seems a particularly big ask, does it?

When President Ike Eisenhower had to deploy paratroopers with bayonets fixed* to escort nine kids into school in Little Rock in 1957, it suddenly sounds like a bad dream.

When Rosa Parks didn't want to move seats on her bus, that doesn't sound like a good dream either – it's a seat on a bus. No one wants to be on a bus. You'd only fight over a seat in a nightmare.

Fourteen-year-old Emmett Till went into a shop. That got him murdered. The killers weren't convicted and confessed later. He went into a shop. That's it. No one dreams of going into a shop.

In a country that – let's be honest now – sells itself as a democracy and the home of freedom, you'd think people would be able to vote. No one dreams of voting; they just expect to be able to do it in a democracy. You wouldn't dream you'd have to march like they did in Selma for the right to vote, let alone get beaten up by police for marching for the right to vote, in a democracy.

Martin Luther King also never dreamt he'd be shot for wanting kids to go to school, get on the bus, or vote either.

---

* He sent in the 101st Airborne Division (that's right, *Band of Brothers*) who amongst other things had landed on D-DAY as well as captured HITLER's house at the end of the war.

Right from the start of the Fifties, black people in the US fought for the mundane, the ordinary, the entirely boring things that white people took for granted.

CIVIL RIGHTS MOVEMENT QUIZ:

Q. Why were people not allowed to go to school, take the bus, go in a shop, vote, live somewhere, get married, etc. etc.?

A. Not because of their race, because of racists.

The Fifties and Sixties saw the start of a titanic ongoing struggle by and for black people in the USA to be allowed to be boring, mundane, usual, rather than the phantom imaginings and ludicrous projections of racists who a) really think this stuff and b) really don't like it if you point out that they're racists. Work in progress.

Women get an Ism

The Sixties also saw the growth of the Women's Liberation movement, or Women's Lib as it was called mainly by freaking-out men. This was the birth of Feminism, accompanied by the crucial discovery of the existence of sexism, which it turned out, like America or Australia, had always been there.

Women had finally, in the century of -isms, finally gone and got themselves an -ism, which on the face of it, given the total disaster all the other -isms had been, might not sound like a good thing. But your author is the father to three daughters and can't find a way to adopt a cynical attitude to Feminism especially not with one of them reading this book over his shoulder as he writes it.

Like the Civil Rights Movement, Feminists wanted lots of boring ordinary things, like the vote, like better pay, like making their own decisions about how they might live their lives, generally being treated with respect, and all the boring stuff that wasn't much on offer, unless of course you count someone holding a door open for you. Which is also nice, obviously, but I'm not sure it quite makes up for the right to do what you want with your own body.

A lot of this seemed to coincide with the invention of SEX, so needless to say lots of men got confused and the confused men got hung up on the business of Feminists burning their bras. Bra burning was a gesture of defiance about the way women's fashions were sexualised and idealised: lots of men thought 'Ooh boobies!', proving the point somewhat.

During the Seventies, Feminism did everything it could to try to get men to shut up about bra burning, but the memory ran deep. Men love bras – the horror of witnessing bras, as they saw it, needlessly destroyed, led them to overlook that without bras breasts were more on show, not less. Mind you, they were just as confused by the idea that women might want to dress any way they liked which could easily mean wearing less. Perhaps when you're so readily distracted by the mental cry of 'Ooh! Boobies!' these things do become pretty complicated.

It is therefore understandable that some Feminists declared themselves against men in general given that the main counter-argument to Feminism amounted to 'Ooh boobies!'.

Talk of women having orgasms also distracted men from taking any of it that seriously.

Changes came (and keep coming) in increments, mainly because the Feminist movement didn't give up, weren't deterred and gradually chipped away at the things they wanted: rights for women, healthcare and all the boring stuff that in general men had expected for themselves.

Cars and work featured in Feminism to some extent. For instance in 1968 the women who made seat covers for Ford motors in Dagenham went on strike because they weren't paid as well as the skilled men. While this got made into a heart-warming family-friendly movie with Bob Hoskins in it, the women at the time were genuinely taking on the world, and the law was changed in 1970.

In the USA in the 1990s leading Feminists Thelma and Louise changed everything for women in the US by driving off a cliff in a car. At least that's what people seemed to think at the time. Sometimes I'm just reporting this stuff.

Housework – long the expected task of women, even working women – started to be something men would have to do, though not without a ton of pointless bitching about it – and to be honest, I love gadgets so I'll hoover. And changing nappies too, what's wrong with you if you won't do that, fellas?

Feminism has gone through several waves, which like any proper Revolution involved the new generation forgetting and/or denouncing those that had gone before them. Women's pay improved, though probably not as much as it could, women's health became a thing, but let's not get too excited about any of that eh?

By the Nineties, Feminism had become so mainstream that Feminists were even forming pop groups and reaching the top of the charts, most notably the Spice Girls, whose work educating the public with regards to the different strands of Third Wave Feminism remains unmatched, especially their understanding of the different categories of Feminist thought around class (Posh Spice), child rearing (Baby Spice), male misogyny (Scary Spice), representation of women in sport (Sporty Spice) and there was Ginger Spice as well on miscellaneous.

ENGLAND WIN THE WORLD CUP, 1966

Now, here's the thing.

Throughout this book I have suggested that some things were a long time ago and best not worried about, and that frankly what can you do about it anyway? It's not like you did it, and it's not like it was done to you. Hey: move on. It's History; literally, History. However. Here's an event that is truly epochal. That burns bright more than half a century after it happened. That is fondly remembered and hailed by men and women born long after it took place. That also set a very, very high bar. But don't worry about it. At least on this one there's no danger of it being the biggest British humiliation since Suez.

Key facts

England played West Germany.
Venue: Wembley Stadium.
England manager: Alf Ramsey.

England team: Gordon Banks, George Cohen, Jack Charlton, Bobby Moore (captain), Ray Wilson, Nobby Stiles, Alan Ball, Bobby Charlton, Martin Peters, Geoff Hurst, Roger Hunt.

Germany team: Don't worry about it.

Score: At full time it was 2–2. Don't worry about it.

Score at the end of extra time: 4–2, proving conclusively that England crushed Germany brilliantly.

Linesman controversy?: Don't worry about it.

Number of times Germany has won the World Cup since: Three.

Number of times England has won the World Cup since: Don't worry about it.

Impact

It's not every piece of History that actually gets remembered.
The England World Cup win in 1966 is unusual for being one
of them, and also for not being about politics, war, chaos, etc.

Whatever else was going on in the Sixties – and there was
plenty of stuff as I hope I've made clear in these pages – it's
1966 that a lot of people would rather talk about. And fair
enough. After all, a win is a win, even if it's the linesman that
wins it for you (see 'Linesman controversy'?).

Most importantly

The World Cup 'Jules Rimet' trophy was then stolen from where it was displayed in Westminster and found by a dog named Pickles in South London a week later.

That is how much winning the World Cup meant to people in England at the time whatever anyone tells you.

Pickles went on to become a presenter on *Match of the Day* and backstage interviewer for *One Man And His Dog* until his death in 1973.

THE VIETNAM WAR, 1955–1975

While the COLD WAR was all about there being no war in Europe, the USSSRRRRRRRRR or USA, it blew up elsewhere. US political wisdom entertained a notion called domino theory: if one country fell to communist influence then so would the one next to it and so on. So while the British, French, Dutch were doing everything – and I mean *everything* – they could to get out of foreign Imperial entanglements, the Americans were getting gleefully stuck in.

The Korean War – 25 June 1950 to 27 July 1953 (though technically it's still going, by the way) – left 3 million Koreans dead as well as tens of thousands of Americans, Chinese and everyone else who mucked in, but what it did do was stop COMMUNISM in its tracks. Right there, halfway down Korea.

Korea was cut in half, because that had turned out so well with Germany, and the northern communist bit was left to get on with it. The Korean War is always a bit of a footnote.*

---

* Footnote.

Au revoir, à bientôt, nous sommes hors d'ici

At the same time, the French had been fighting the communist-backed Viet Minh in its former colony Vietnam; by the time the French had been evicted, the American government offered to help the south of the country* repel the Chinese-backed communist north.

The French army withdrew to make a terrible mess of things in Algeria instead.

'Advice'

Back in Vietnam, the Americans at first didn't send soldiers. Hell no, they were there as advisers: 'Ooh no, I wouldn't do that if I were you, oh well too late.'

In 1964, there were 23,000 advisers in Vietnam. That's a hell of a lot of advice, most of it bad, judging how things turned out.

As the war grew and the North Vietnamese army and the Việt Cong (guerrilla forces) proved hard to beat, more and more advisers were sent and then eventually the actual American army turned up to take their own advice. They then demonstrated that

---

* It had also been cut in two because that always makes things so much easier to deal with.

maybe the advice they'd been doling out wasn't that good, as they bombed, blasted, flattened, torched and poisoned the place. 'It became necessary to destroy the town to save it,' as a US major remarked afterwards.

A huge effort went into winning over hearts and minds in Vietnam as well as bombing the country to hell and back. They possibly contradicted each other. Hard to say.

The Vietnam War was one of the first wars to be televised, but at a much slower turnover than in current times: that meant if you saw something horrendous on the TV the chances are it would be shown again and again. Then it became the fodder for movies, mainly films in which Americans got grumpy and upset about how sad it made them to flatten a country when there didn't seem to be any point flattening the country. I know, right?

Nam, maN

If the SUEZ CRISIS was the worst thing that ever happened to British foreign policy and remained the gold-standard screw-up for the UK, then the Vietnam War was for America a billion Suez Crises squared. For decades, everything the US did was compared to Vietnam, and for generations it was clear that there was no way American politics or society could possibly get over it. Movies would feature characters who'd been in Vietnam to save having to write them personalities. ('You weren't there, man!')

213

America threw its weight around for scant reward, propped up the South Vietnamese government for zero thanks, blasted and bombed three countries for more than a decade, lost tens of thousands of soldiers, killed many more, conscription exacerbated racial tensions at home and deepened civil rights divisions, and then it was all OK because Sylvester Stallone blew up Steven Berkoff in *Rambo II*.

There was no way whatsoever the Americans could ever top Vietnam. They'd learned their lesson and they'd learned it good: getting involved in foreign wars just wasn't worth the effort, no way. Enough of that. 'You weren't there, man!'

THE MOON LANDINGS, 1969

As the COLD WAR got properly underway between the Americans and the Soviets, it became clear that both superpowers needed an outlet that wouldn't necessarily result in the planet being reduced to cinders.

The space race timeline: it is exactly rocket science

1942 The Germans put a rocket called the V-2 into space thanks to the efforts of Wernher von Braun, though he is trying to land them on earth not the moon, more specifically London, while full of explosives.

1945 WERWERTWO ends and the Americans and Soviets round up as many German rocket scientists as they possibly can to get them to work for them. The Americans strike gold and recruit von Braun, somehow ignoring his past making Nazi rockets.

1945–1957 The Americans and the Soviets work hard on developing rockets that can deliver nuclear weapons via space because the Soviets and the Americans are working hard on developing rockets that can deliver nuclear weapons via space. Going to actual space has nothing to do with it.

4 October 1957 The Soviets change tack completely and launch a satellite into space. A metal football called *Sputnik 1* goes around the earth bleeping and suddenly it occurs to everyone that you could put something other than a bomb on top of one of these rockets and send it into space: a dog, fruit flies, chimps, even a human being. America goes into full panic mode and two months later tries to launch its own satellite on a Vanguard rocket. It blows up. America panics some more.

1958 The Soviets launch a series of probes at the moon, but miss, somehow. In the US the Americans set up NASA, with the specific aim of getting space stuff underway properly.

1959 Success! The Soviets send a probe around the moon, revealing its dark side, which looks much like the other side. Worth every rouble.

1961 GAGARIN! The Soviets beat the Americans to it a second time and launch a man into orbit around the earth. Cosmonaut Yuri Gagarin flies around the earth in 108 minutes, shorter than most movies but instantly more famous than any actor. The Americans are so embarrassed by this that J. F. Kennedy is bounced into declaring that NASA will put a man on the moon (and bring him back). Billions of dollars of embarrassment there.

1960s The decade of the space race, providing Americans with ten years' worth of small talk to keep their minds off Vietnam or the CIVIL RIGHTS MOVEMENT; as the VIETNAM WAR gets worse and demands for change increase, so NASA responds with bigger and better rockets, more astronauts, and ultimately the grand climax – the Apollo Moon Landings.

Apollo 11: man on the moon, 20 July 1969

Buzz Aldrin and Neil Armstrong (not to forget whatsisname* in the command module) got to the moon after a four-day trip to get there. Their spaceship had been perfected and tested over and over again; a trip had recently been to the moon and back but not landed, an experience usually confined to the world of dating.

On disembarking from the lunar lander, the *Eagle*, Neil Armstrong fluffed his lines on live TV†, which proves conclusively

---

* You know, thingy. Ah come on. Michael Collins, that's it.
† 'One small step for a man, one giant leap for mankind' was what he was meant to say but instead he said, 'One small step for man, one giant leap for mankind.' If he'd remembered the 'a' we wouldn't be talking about it now, would we?

the landings weren't faked like that bloke in the pub says they were: if it had been faked they'd have made him do it again, and then watched the mistakes at the office party on a blooper reel.

Man had got to the moon. Apollo 12 went a few weeks later and no one cared. Apollo 13 went wrong and was rescued thanks to Tom Hanks' insouciant decision-making and low-key grit, and not one soul gave a damn. Try as it might, the space race didn't generate as much small talk as predicted.

The Soviets congratulated the US on landing on the moon then acted like they'd never been trying in the first place.

LESSON FROM HISTORY

Go to the moon by all means, just don't expect anyone to be impressed/believe you.

CAMBODIA:
GIVING COMMUNISM A BAD NAME

One of the consequences of the Vietnam War and its overspill was the Revolution in Cambodia and the arrival on the scene of the Communist government of Pol Pot. American bombers had killed tens of thousands of people trying to stop the North Vietnamese forces from using Cambodia as a short cut to South Vietnam.

The Cambodian government collapsed defeated, even though the war hadn't been against them, and then the various communist Revolutionaries who'd been exiled in France and elsewhere returned to Cambodia to bring about yet another Workers' Paradise. The Cambodia Royal family tried to style it out and hang onto power but quickly found out they were up against something new.

Pol Pot and the gang were going to do it differently: they'd decided that where all the other great Communist Revolutions had gone wrong was in trying to skip straight to being industrial Workers' Paradises. Instead they were going to go back to first principles and go agricultural and rebuild society from scratch.

So what Pol Pot did was evacuate the capital city Phnom Penh, pitting rural Cambodia against its urban population, and then ruthlessly purged anyone who:

a) disagreed
b) looked like they might disagree
c) looked like they might even think about disagreeing
d) had anything to do with the way society had been run before: teachers, academics, business and management types, etc. etc.
e) all of the above.

Phnom Penh was emptied. The world looked on astonished, aghast, but no one outside Cambodia really knew what was going on.

Announcing YEAR ZERO, the start of the everything – from – scratch policy, Pol Pot's government and the Communist Party of Kampuchea. a.k.a. the Khmer Rouge, then set about starving the population of Cambodia to death, deliberately and accidentally, collectivising farming while not knowing that much about farming as well as being very bad at receiving bad news about low crop yields. Families were broken up. People were denounced, processed and murdered. Millions died, maybe a quarter of the country's population, and an entire class of people were wiped out.

What was truly remarkable about the Khmer Rouge's time in power in Cambodia is that lots of other Communist governments thought that they were giving Communism a bad name* and were damaging its reputation†. In the end it took the Vietnamese government – that had just defeated the Americans in the Vietnam War, to overthrow the Khmer Rouge in 1979, which confused the USA no end because both governments were Communist and it couldn't properly pick a side. Pol Pot and the Khmer Rouge faded into the Cambodia country and avoided justice and the country has since done everything it can to piece itself back together and move on.

---

* I know, right?
† Seriously, wtf?

DECIMALISATION:
POUNDS, SHILLINGS AND PENCE, 1971

The many twists and turns of the Twentieth Century can be explained – if you've drunk enough coffee – entirely in terms of economics.

This is all the more remarkable when you consider that the British economy was running on a system of money that no one understood. And by no one, I really do actually mean no one.

It wasn't until money went decimal in 1971 – you know, 100 pence in a pound – that the British public realised they hadn't understood money all along. The result was chaos.

Causes

So: what you had was the pound (£) at the top of the system. One pound was the single largest denomination except for the guinea, which was more than a pound and used to buy horses/ humiliate people bad at mental arithmetic.

- One pound was made up of 720 pennies, or maybe 560 shillings – it's hard to tell – which in turn had 17 crots to the greengage.
- A greengage wasn't the same as a greengang which was worth 11 ha'pennies or 5½ pennies, also known as a taffet.

Prices would be listed in terms of:

- Pounds, shillings and pence, or
- Crowns (amount undefined), crots and greengages
- Unless you were trading smaller items in taffets on a carteret.

The advantage of the Imperial system of money is that it tied in – via its mathematically flexible use of base 13¼ – to the Imperial measurements system, based as it was on the standard unit of measurement of the nearest pony's back left hoof. As motor cars became more prevalent so using the PBLH as a base unit began to be less reliable: fewer ponies meant fewer hoofs.

The Imperial measurement system similarly worked by equating its units of measurement to common things. It included:

- The mile: a long way
- Bloody miles: even further
- A yard: the size of a very small back garden, but big enough for the pony (see pony's back left hoof)

- Inch – the distance travelled by an inchworm in half a minute or half your thumb, whichever is longer
- Furlong: got its name from the expression 'go for long' so about that length, right?
- Crab: the width of a crab, used for measuring crabs
- A pound – weight – completely unrelated to the pound – money

With this system, the British won two world wars. Economists in the late Sixties considered that had the British Chancellors of the Exchequer been using a metric system, WERWERTWO may well have been up to a year and a half shorter. So the government led by Harold Wilson (gimmick: pipe, northern, bit bonkers) decided that it was done with crots and crabs and taffets, and brought in the much easier to use decimal system – 100 pennies in the pound and 100 grams in the kilogram, etc.

Effects

It was for this reason and this reason only that the 1970s were such a disaster: everyone was trying to figure out how much money they had now that the system had changed.

Reasons

However, what Wilson forgot is that the old system was laid down by King Arthur himself and Alfred the Great by Merlin the Magician as instructed by Jesus when he visited Tintagel in AD30. And by getting rid of it, Wilson broke the link with the Eternal Ancient Island Magick and as result nothing has been as good since.[*]

---

[*] Just don't try paying for this book in taffets.

RACE TO THE BOTTOM

DISCLAIMER! THE AUTHOR HAS CHECKED HIS WHITE PRIVILEGE AND IT IS IN FULL WORKING ORDER.

Following WERWERTWO, the British economy needed workers. With the British Empire coming to the end of its use-by date, workers from the rest of the world were seen as the answer.

In 1948, the *Empire Windrush* brought a consignment of passengers from Jamaica. Some of them were looking for jobs back in the services like they'd had during the war. It wasn't until 1962 that the British government stopped people simply coming into the UK from its colonies.

Indian and Pakistani people also came to the UK, mainly to get away from Pakistan and India. Or India and Pakistan. Bangladeshis also came, to get away from Bangladesh, or India. Chinese people fled the communist Revolution. Asians from Uganda, when they were thrown out by Idi Amin's regime in

1972, also came to the UK. Of course: it's the greatest country in the world! Who wouldn't want to come here?

Reasons to come to Britain included:

1. Work, though not the kind of work British people wanted to do;
2. Housing, though not the kind of housing British people wanted;
3. Freedom to live your life the way you wanted, though actually probably not really;
4. A warm welcome, though not the kind of welcome British people would put up with for one second.

They got all four!

A day at the racists

Immigrants faced racism and discrimination wherever they went – in the workplace, their neighbourhoods and their kids in schools. Racism expressed itself in different ways: low pay, poor conditions, violence, bullying, casual stereotyping.

To help all this along, firebrand Tory MP and self-styled radical thinker* Enoch Powell intervened. Powell was an ambitious man and could fashion an argument out of any old dog-end.

---

* Avoid! Avoid!

Even though he had made a name for himself in WERW-ERTWO fighting racists, i.e. the Nazis, Powell decided that all this disparate and different British racism at grassroots level simply wasn't good enough, and took it on himself to bring it into mainstream politics at the highest level. He did this with a speech in 1968 that a) got him sacked b) he doesn't get a b).

Powell was reacting to Harold Wilson's Labour government introducing the Race Relations Act, which made it illegal to discriminate on racial grounds, what with it being wrong. Sometimes you have to write laws like that. Powell objected to the act on moral grounds, somehow.

Powell – who was regarded certainly by himself as the cleverest man ever to live* – did what anyone who reckons they're clever would do and used references to classical Rome to make his point. It always wins people over. Quoting Virgil, never fails. He described himself as 'like the Roman' though he can't have meant that he cleaned his teeth with twigs and urine.†
He said he saw 'the River Tiber foaming with much blood' which, given he was speaking in Wolverhampton, suggested he had powerful binoculars.

---

* Powell claimed to have taught himself fifty-eight languages in a weekend or something.

† On reflection that could explain his permanently sour expression.

Fact!

When making a speech, Powell would deliberately not go to the toilet to give himself that particularly urgent air. It also possibly explained why he was so full of shit.

Powell's speech went down well with the public, in particular the trades union movement who hadn't yet got the memo about anti-racism – as they saw it, they were protecting their members' jobs from black and brown people, for white people. The Tory Party in some sort of mirror-universe moment ditched Powell, for ever.*

The scene was set for tedious old people who should know better to invoke the name of the toilet-dodging rabble-rouser for the next few decades.

Multiculturalism

Post-Powell racists in general wised up to the idea that racism was bad and declared they wouldn't ever want to be called racist while carrying on being racist. To combat this, the idea of multiculturalism emerged: a hare-brained and half-crazed notion that everyone should just try to get along. Apart from the racists.

---

* He joined the Ulster Unionists for light relief.

The Seventies, Eighties, Nineties and beyond were an endless grinding game of racial snakes and ladders. Prejudice and injustice chipped away, reinforced, overturned, every generation back on square one.

On 19 May 2018, the twists and turns of racism versus multiculturalism culminated in the Royal family doing the previously unthinkable and allowing a ginger person to get married, something no one would ever have predicted in the bad old days of the Seventies.

NORTHERN IRELAND:
THEY CALLED IT 'THE TROUBLES'.
THEY WEREN'T JOKING

MEANWHILE:

In Northern Ireland, splitting the island of Ireland into two was working its sweet magic of peace, love and harmony.

It's all pretty simple though as long as you bear in mind that: the Catholics hated the Protestants who hated the Nationalists who hated the Loyalists who hated the Republicans who hated the RUC who hated the IRA who hated the British army who hated the INLA who hated the UDA who hated OIRA who hated the UVF who hated the IPLO who hated the LVF who hated the Catholics and round again please. Amongst the Loyalists were people so loyal to Britain they were prepared to fight the British army. You know the type.

Like everything else in Ulster, there is no agreement about when The Troubles started.

The end of the Sixties saw an escalation in violence between communities in Northern Ireland that focused around Catholics wanting dull boring things like the vote, housing and jobs. There was rioting, fighting, escalation. Firebombing, people killed.

By the end of the 1960s, the British army had been deployed to be shot at, blown up and have stuff thrown at it. Always good to involve the army in this sort of thing.

Key events and contributory factors: all of Irish History preceding this moment

- **Internment:** In August 1971, the British army decided the best way to demonstrate British values of fair play and due process was to arrest and imprison without trial the people it thought were wrong 'uns. This went down as well as you might expect seeing as it relied on military intelligence. Coupled with a curfew the previous month, it ensured the British army would most definitely be shot at, blown up and have stuff thrown at it.
- **Bloody Sunday:** On 30 January 1972, a protest march for Catholic civil rights turned into a chance for paratroopers to run around Londonderry shooting people. Fourteen people died. Later Bono got to prop up the Irish economy with a hit record of the same name.
- **Pub bombings:** In 1974, the IRA murdered British civilians in England, blowing up pubs in Guildford

and Birmingham. Who blows up pubs? In two-wrongs style, the police did everything they could to ensure British values of fair play and due process were upheld by arresting whoever they could get their hands on and fitting them up for the bombings.

- **Hunger strikes, bombings, shootings, riots, marches, more bombings, fat ranty vicars, thin intense priests, handwringing politicians, actors having their voices dubbed onto the IRA's spokesmen,** etc.

The 1970s and 1980s were two long, grim decades of bombings, assassinations, the army being shot at, blown up and having stuff thrown at it, and the army shooting back, blowing stuff up but not so much throwing things. Hunger strikes, bombings, shootings. As murdering scumbag bastards go, the IRA were pretty successful. As well as killing hundreds of ordinary people they got high-profile targets too: Lord Louis Mountbatten and the Conservative Party conference were both blown up, as well as Harrods and Hyde Park. Their loyalist opposite numbers were similarly murderous.

You can't really pick a side in this one. Except perhaps unless you're one of the poor sods being blown up, shot at, etc.

What's important is that in 'the mainland' the whole business of Northern Ireland was misunderstood and, if at all possible, ignored. So, seeing as I can't get my head round it, that's enough of that.

SOMETHING JOHNNY ROTTEN
IN THE STATE OF ENGLAND

Pop music in the 1970s changed fashion every five minutes. In the first five years of the Seventies you had tons of styles. Different bands, different artists, each distinct and unique in its own style:

- **Prog rock:** long guitar solos, capes, keyboards, spaceships, extravagant staging;
- **Glam rock:** capes, keyboards, spaceships, extravagant staging, long guitar solos;
- **Art rock:** keyboards, spaceships, long guitar solos, capes, extravagant staging;
- **David Bowie:** spaceships, extravagant staging, capes, long guitar solos, keyboards;
- **Heavy metal:** long guitar solos, keyboards, spaceships, extravagant staging, capes;
- **Heavy rock:** see above.

Everyone bought records with the money they would have bought video games with if there had been video games. By the middle of the Seventies, a reaction to all the different styles and their different music was due.

Along came the punks! Johnny Rotten, Sid Vicious, Bob Nasty, Ray Bang! and Gerald Collins formed the Sex* Pistols in 1975 and their style blew the world apart. They understood that pop music required a gimmick: their gimmick was to have no gimmicks. At least not gimmicks they would have to spend money on. Aided by Malcolm McLaren, who ran a newsagent's, (might have been a shoe shop, not sure) and his partner Vivienne Westwood, who would wear black bin bags and paper bags as hats, they shot to fame like a meteor.

Because they were broke working-class lads from London, they couldn't afford capes, keyboards, extravagant staging, spaceships – nor could they afford guitars, so long guitar solos were out of the question. Making a virtue of a necessity, the Sex Pistols made a big thing of how they couldn't play their instruments. They possibly didn't own any?

They took the world by storm. Going on the telly and swearing was an affordable gimmick the Sex Pistols made the most of: young people all over the country were stunned by the swearing and the lack of capes, etc.

Johnny Rotten specialised in flicking Vs at anyone who

---

* By this point in the Seventies, SEX was becoming commonplace.

he could flick Vs at and pearls were clutched the length and breadth of the country.

Immediately, punks all over the world glued their hair into Mohicans, wore safety pins as earrings, dressed up in bin bags and just like Elvis before them they brought down not only music but civilisation itself. From the shattered ruins of the music industry, overwhelmed by the punk onslaught, ABBA and Boney M sold 30 million records anyway like it hadn't happened.

BRITAIN JOINS THE EEC, 1973

Nothing to see here. Move along. Probably happened by accident.

UP TO AND INCLUDING
THE WINTER OF DISCONTENT, 1978–9

———————————

The Tory PM Edward Heath (gimmick: sailing, conducting orchestras, thinking Europe was fine, really) had come undone dealing with industrial strife. The 1970s had been characterised by industrial strife. The pattern was as follows:

- **Tory government:** unions condemn the Tories as class-war enemies, demand higher pay.
- **Labour government:** unions condemn the Labour government for betraying their class-war allies, demand higher pay. (Labour governments seemed to suffer even more in dealing with industrial disputes: they were meant to be on the same side, after all.)

Added to this the country still couldn't figure out the new decimal money: the fifty-pence piece with its seven sides was a horrifically modern affront to all sensible people and the country went on strike every three weeks as a result.

Heath called an election in 1974 to try to show the unions who was boss: the slogan was 'Who governs?' and it turned out it wasn't Edward Heath. Harold Wilson took up the mantle of government again for Labour then kindly passed it on to Jim Callaghan when it all got too much. It was Jim Callaghan who ended up trying to sort things out with the unions from the left once and for all and the Winter of Discontent – nothing to do with disco – had the nation in its grip.

On Jim's watch by the end of the 1970s strikes were happening every seven or eight minutes: a billion working hours were lost a week and over the winter of 1978/9, dead people had to bury themselves and rats drove the bin lorries.

THE THATCHER YEARS, THE 1980S

With the Seventies groaning to a heaving halt – and when you look at the footage the Seventies was a decade perfectly suited to being filmed in lurid, fuzzy, grimy colour – the Labour government under Jim Callaghan staggered along like a man with his trousers round his knees, his drawers flapping in the breeze.

This was the golden age of Britain being the 'Sick Man of Europe'. You couldn't move for opinions along these lines. Governments both Labour and Tory had slithered from disaster to disaster, the electorate let them know how crap they thought they were by never quite giving them proper majorities, and there was a general feeling of stagnation, frustration, impotence and all the stuff you might feel before making a big hasty decision.

So the stage was set for the general election in May 1979: the Conservatives under TheThatcher, despite her reputation for stealing all the milk in the UK from all of the country's children* when she was education secretary, won a 43-seat majority.

---

* Give or take.

So began TheThatcherYears.

TheThatcherYears saw, the country torn in two/everything get better/turn to shit/not be as good as the old days/not be as bad as what went before it. Look, there was tons for people to complain about.*

In other words: buckle in! This one's controversy-packed! No one's gonna like it!

Chiefly, the main thing to remember about TheThatcher is she drove everyone insane. Crackers. Barking mad. Stark staring. Howling. Bonkers. Moon-wailing.

It was a time characterised by madness. And there was no one TheThatcher didn't get to.

1. Her opponents were driven to total distraction by her, and as a result made a series of self-crushing errors that she was able to exploit. Many are still driven mad by her, fixated on TheThatcher long after it shuffled off.

2. Her supporters also were driven stark staring mad by her, at the time struck insane by her manner, her character and very often the fact that she was a woman telling them what to do. And the further into time TheThatcher has receded, the madder it has made them. People now, decades later, calling themselves Thatcherite are similarly doolally.

---

* This may be the point.

These people are dazzled by her forthright style and ignorant of the way TheThatcher often decided to compromise but liked to act as though compromise wasn't an option ('U-turn if you want to, the lady's not for turning'). The bit for which they love her most is when TheThatcher finally succumbed to the spell as well, and went utterly spare, crashing around annoying everyone, i.e. the time when she blew it over Europe and the poll tax.

TheThatcher regarded the post-war settlement – nationalised industries, subsidies from government, etc/ – as uncompetitive and stifling to the economy. TheThatcher thought that cutting the purse strings of the state would solve all of the country's problems, which when you think about it for even the shortest amount of time, was bound to upset a lot of people. Lots of them in the Tory Party, whom TheThatcher called Wets. The Wets tried to restrain TheThatcher, doing what they could to sidetrack policy, which was the best way possible to wind TheThatcher up. They were driven mad by TheThatcher; TheThatcher was driven mad by them.

The Iranian Embassy siege, 1980

In 1979, Iran, which up until then had been a friend of the West largely thanks to the West backing a government that was selling the West its oil and buying the West's planes, suddenly underwent a change of management. Now the Islamic Revolution under the Ayatollah Khomeini was underway and

Iran rejected the West, its planes and oil sales. This Revolution did the thing Revolutions usually do and started for one reason – either dissatisfaction with the status quo, the ruling family, or perceived outside interference, choose according to taste – and ended up somewhere else altogether.

One of the stranger side Effects of this colossal event was the Iranian Embassy siege of 1980. Sworn enemies of the Khomeini regime, the Democratic* Revolutionary† Front‡ for the Liberation§ of Arabistan¶ seized the Iranian Embassy in Kensington, just along the road from the Royal Albert Hall. Embassies featured large in the Iranian Revolution – the US Embassy in Tehran and its occupants had been held hostage by Revolutionaries in 1979 for over a year and the US had botched an attempt to rescue them, which would have been their greatest humiliation since Suez if they were British. That bad.

Seizing the Iranian Embassy in London, the Democratic Revolutionary Front issued the standard demands of the time: release certain prisoners we want to free or the hostages get it. Given that the new Iranian government wasn't big on sympathy this seemed unlikely. And the DRFLA had not reckoned with

---

* Probably not.

† Definitely.

‡ Is six people a Front? Probably not, but you might not want to argue the toss if it was your building they burst into.

§ Cool, if you say so.

¶ 'New phone, where's that?'

TheThatcher who, rather than settling for the Iranian regime's enemies being TheThatcher's friends, decided that this sort of thing could not be tolerated on British soil.

This meant one thing: after a period of tedious negotiation via megaphone and telephone and stale sandwiches and demands being read out on the telly, TheThatcher decided to send in the SAS. This decision was precipitated on the fifth day of the siege by the terrorists killing one of the hostages and throwing their body out of the embassy.

The SAS, you need to know, are the most glamorous crack outfit of soldiers on the planet bar none. Given how glamorous they are, it's odd to think they'd been almost completely forgotten when the siege took place, live on TV. They interrupted the snooker: men in black outfits with gas masks on, setting fire to the curtains at the embassy. The SAS managed, despite a prediction that they might kill 40 per cent of the hostages, only to kill one, which you have to agree is a result.

It's not known how many soldiers were involved in the abseiling, smashing-in, terrorist-shooting, hostage-avoiding and curtain-burning but it put the SAS firmly in the public eye.

The whole episode made TheThatcher look decisive and tough, though definitely not as decisive and tough as if it had been her bursting into the embassy and setting fire to the curtains. Mind you, people still seemed to think she was somehow miraculously responsible for the whole thing.

Iranian Embassy siege key facts

1. Everyone has forgotten who the terrorists were and what they were doing because they got upstaged. Moral: if you're a terrorist group don't get upstaged.
2. The SAS were top secret until they went on the telly. Moral: don't go on the telly if you're top secret.
3. Within weeks you could buy an Action Man in the SAS black outfit with a gas mask. The SAS couldn't do anything about it because they were top secret.

The Iran-Iraq War then started, which was:

4. A long way away;
5. Too bleak to interrupt the snooker for (and went on for years so it would have disrupted the snooker schedule too much);
6. A bit complicated and tough to pick a side you'd want to win.

So everyone forgot all about the reasons for the siege even if they knew them in the first place.

And now we come to the bit we all love: economics

TheThatcherYears started with her Chancellor of the Exchequer, Geoffrey Howe, trying to 'reduce the money supply'. This was based on the principle of cutting your kids' pocket money to get them to spend it more wisely, I think.

Either way, it's one of those political (often economic) things that comes up in History, which the politicians grasp onto, make everyone talk about to the exclusion of all else and then forget instantly when it doesn't seem to be working out for them. Others include:

1. Appeasement. Sorry, no, nothing to do with me.
2. The poll tax.
3. The Iraq War (Iraq War Two that is).
4. Austerity, which it turns out was no one's idea and anyway what are you talking about?
5. *
6. †

This was an example of an economic theory in action called 'monetarism' and because you're not an idiot you immediately know that economic theories put into action tend not to be all they're cracked up to be. Very often they have unforeseen consequences. 'Reducing the money supply' had the not altogether unsurprising effect of 'reducing the workforce'. Unemployment went up quicker than a plane pulling out of a dive. TheThatcher reassured the public that this meant it was working. Certainly,

---

* I've left this blank for the next one that we run into.

† And this one. Come on, this happens all the time.

fewer people working meant they had less money to spend and the money supply was thus reduced. It has its own logic, doesn't it?

Further economic tinkering – putting VAT up on everything – had the stunningly unpredictable effect of making everything more expensive. If your economic theory involves putting the price of everything up, it might not be very tactful to act indignant when inflation follows. But that was TheThatcher. TheThatcher government then did everything it could to bring inflation back down again like it had happened out of nowhere and was nothing to do with them.

During her first term, TheThatcher tended to propose one thing and end up doing another. Proposing a cut in public spending of 1 per cent, but it actually went up. Irony ruled. TheThatcher believed in law and order, so there were riots in Brixton and Toxteth.

The government reduced the number of people it was employing in nationalised industries which – get this! – caused unemployment to go up. I have no training in economics – as I stated before, it's my considered view that economists are simply the most resistant to falling asleep when faced with economics – but I reckon I could have worked that one out. Unemployment went up to levels not seen since the GREAT DEPRESSION, but TheThatcher remained resolute. Besides, lots of unemployed people was helping to keep the inflation down, which had gone up.

The opposition

Not wanting to miss out on the action, the Labour Party reacted to TheThatcher by tearing itself in two and installing Michael Foot as its leader, who was an old-school Labour politician not unlike the people who had failed the country and the party in the 1970s. This wasn't good enough for the likes of Tony Benn, who attempted to unseat him from the left.

Another chunk of the Labour Party, well, just four of them at first (including top Labour reformer Roy Jenkins), left to form the Social Democratic Party, which was seen by many on the left as the ultimate betrayal (honestly, this is a whole book if that's your thing but mercifully it isn't the one I've been asked to write). They spent the rest of TheThatcherYears being blamed by the Labour Party either for splitting or for not having stayed, which are of course the same thing but sometimes politics is all about the tautology.

TheThatcher also tried to take on trades unions where it could find them, and as the first term continued it sank further and further into unpopularity. By the start of 1982, TheThatcher was tanking in the polls. It took outside intervention to rescue TheThatcher from obscurity. And in 1982 that's exactly what came along.

THE FALKLANDS WAR, 1982:
UK – STILL GOT IT

If, at the start of 1982, you had sat down next to anyone in the UK and said, 'This year there will be a war between the UK and Argentina over the Falkland Islands and the UK will win,' they would have moved further down the carriage, or given you the look of the pitied. Had you persisted and followed them down the carriage and somehow managed to get them to engage in the conversation, they'd have doubtless revealed that a) they didn't know where the Falklands were and b) actually, sorry, no they'd never heard of them. They probably knew no more than that Argentina had a nifty football team, like a less enjoyable Brazil. But war?

The Falklands War, which lasted barely three months from start to finish, took everyone by surprise: the British, the Argentinians, the Falkland Islanders, the penguins.

Would this event be the biggest British humiliation since SUEZ?

Causes

- Tiny islands, middle of nowhere, scrambled egg on the map.
- On a globe, close to South America, though still around 300 miles away. Not that this makes much odds if you think that they belong to Argentina because they're nearest to Argentina, but that argument means that the UK might make claim to vast chunks of Western Europe, in particular Ireland. Stop right there, we haven't got time.*
- By the same token, the Falkland Islands are many more than 300 miles from the United Kingdom, so maybe distance isn't the best measurement. Not that I want to get into any of this.

Key points

- The people who lived there were quite clear that they wanted to be British.
- The people who lived next door disagreed.
- It's like one of those disputes neighbours get into about where the fence should go up to. The

---

* See EASTER RISING.

Argentinians thought the fence should go all round
the Falklands.

Anyway, it's not this book's job to get into the rights and
wrongs of it. Though the British colony predates the existence
of Argentina, which itself is a colony. But honestly, I'm not
going to get bogged down in this. Not interested.

Argentinian writer Jorge Luis Borges famously described
the Falklands War as being 'like two bald men fighting over
a comb' (and trust me, he knew what he was talking about),
but sometimes men, bald or otherwise, really want a fight and
really want a comb.

The Conflict/War/Fight over the comb

Short version only: British Task Force sails south, wins improb-
able win.

Effects

The Effects of the Falklands War are probably why what had
happened was so controversial.

1. The following year, 1983, Thatcher won a huge majority
   thanks to what was called 'The Falklands Factor'. Given

her government had been pretty unpopular before the war, politics was turned upside down and TheThatcher was able to pursue her policies with a great big majority and an even bigger head. *The papers love it!*

2. 'Britain is back, baby!' was a feeling that did the rounds, and not just back from the South Atlantic, back in general. Far from being the worst crisis since Suez, it was the best crisis since Suez. *The papers love it!*

3. Shamed by the defeat and humbled on the world stage having failed in a dramatic 'you had one job' style, the hideous Argentine military government fell. Democratic reform followed, and you can't argue with that as an effect no matter how indirect or otherwise. *The papers have lost interest by now!*

4. British people were still not sure where the Falklands were; Argentinian opinion was unmoved on the question of who they belong to.

So: swings and roundabouts you might say* though what you're doing in a playground could be the thing you have to explain.

---

* Though most people forget point 3.

THE MINERS' STRIKE

Top scientist and gravity sage Isaac Newton once posited what would happen if the irresistible force met the immoveable object, but he had never once entered into his calculations the possibility of TheThatcher and Mr Scargill.

The Miners' Strike had its origins in Ted Heath's government's troubles in the Seventies and the GENERAL STRIKE of 1926 if going that far back is to your taste. TheThatcher loathed Ted Heath because he had taken on the miners' unions and lost. She also loathed the miners because they had taken on Ted Heath and won. Anyway, scores to settle. After WERWERTWO, the Attlee government, The-Greatest-Government-There-Ever-Was™, nationalised the coal industry: this was the legacy of 1926. As a result, the government picked up the tab for coal and paid the coalminers' wages. TheThatcher didn't like this one bit.

Some facts about the mining industry in the Eighties:

1. Like in 1926, coal from abroad was cheaper, including from communist COLD WAR enemy Poland. TheThatcher may not have had a sense of humour but she did do irony.
2. Some mines were running out of coal, and this made it even more expensive. The President of the miners' union, Mr Scargill, didn't believe that closing down a mine just because it didn't make any money made any sense.
3. Mining was still a horrible unsafe job that you should be paid a king's ransom for and God knows you wouldn't get me doing it.

The miners were ready for trouble. Mr Scargill had been looking forward to it. If TheThatcher was implacable and armour-plated (nickname: The Iron Lady) then Mr Scargill was the coal-blackened yin to her yang. They were made for each other.

While TheThatcher coldly intoned economic and political theory about why mines were going to have to close, Mr Scargill responded with white-hot boss-class-war rhetoric. All diction: all friction. It was like *Moonlighting*. If the Miners' Strike was a rom-com they'd be snogging at the end. It wasn't a rom-com though. Quite the opposite.

Before the FALKLANDS WAR, TheThatcher had been planning to shut mines, but the unions had threatened to strike and stopped her. Post-Falklands election landslide, TheThatcher

– having dealt with the enemy without, i.e. the Argentinians – switched to what she called the enemy within, the National Union of Mineworkers (NUM).

Furthermore: Mr Scargill was no exception regarding TheThatcher's hypnotic powers and seemed also to be driven quite mad by her. The scene was set.

Key points: smouldering with controversy

- TheThatcher stockpiled coal for power stations, and had made sure the law had been changed to make picketing somewhere you didn't work illegal. The police were organised into mobile squads to respond to picketing. On 6 March 1984, TheThatcher announced that twenty pits would close: 20,000 would go. Mr Scargill said there was a secret plot to close seventy pits.

- TheThatcher was able to frame the strike as democracy (her) versus anti-democracy (Mr Scargill) for one simple reason that totally snookered the Labour Party (led by Neil Kinnock): Mr Scargill had called the strike and not balloted his members first. Well, a Special National Delegate Conference voted on whether there'd be a vote and decided against. Awkward.

Strikes broke out all over. Pickets tried to stop men who'd decided against striking – 'scabs' as they were called – and the police responded. The violence reached its peak at Orgreave in July 1984, with 5,000 striking miners trying to picket a coking plant. A pitched battle took place: policemen on horseback and with riot shields, more men being brought in from all over the country. While the miners were fighting for their jobs, the violence had a dark side: a taxi driver taking strike breakers to work was killed.

Public support slipped away: the public in general felt sorry for the miners but didn't like Mr Scargill much.

As well as fisticuffs, the strike was fought out in the courts: miners who wanted to work took the NUM to court, arguing the strike was illegal. A breakaway union calling itself the Union of Democratic Mineworkers was formed.

The strike dragged on for the rest of the year: many miners who had stayed out were forced back to work out of hunger by the time the winter came.

Result

The immediate result was total defeat for the NUM, Mr Scargill, miners, mining, coal, the whole thing. Even the Union of Democratic Mineworkers faced closures. Victory for TheThatcher. Having relieved the country of the onerous burden of mines that produced expensive coal she left everyone on the dole: to TheThatcher this was a better use of public funds. The only bright side is coal mining is a horrible job, honestly.

Other result

Probably not the result she expected, but TheThatcher now thought she was totally invincible and had political judgement like no other, which she proved by bringing in the poll tax, which – along with fighting over Europe and undermining her Chancellor – destroyed her politically. She drove everyone mad, I tell you.

THE COLD WAR PART 4589: GORBACHEV RIDES TO THE RESCUE

The Soviet Union (remember that?), the USA's great antagonist in the COLD WAR (remember that?), entered the 1980s in full 'same but different' mode. Ideologically opposed to the USA. Entrenched in Eastern Europe, backing the Iron Curtain to the hilt. Backing its friends, allies and clients all over the world. Pointing missiles at its enemies. And up to its neck in it in Afghanistan.

The Soviets had invaded Afghanistan to save the stumbling communist government that had failed to create a Workers' Paradise, probably due to a shortage of workers. Riding to the rescue of the unpopular government was contentious within the Politburo but the Soviets couldn't admit they had made a mistake and withdraw. Pretty soon it became clear that the Russian army, built for sweeping into West Germany as quickly as possible, wasn't well suited to a protracted internal policing job in a country that, at best, resented their presence. Casualties grew and unrest mounted at home. Afghans made do with what weaponry they had, used their local knowledge of the country, as well as getting help from abroad ... look, just stop me if this sounds too familiar, OK? Invading Afghanistan never works out. That must be why people keep doing it.

This put pressure on the USSSSRRRRRRR, which had not quite delivered on the Workers' Paradise it had promised at home either. Sure, everyone had a job, but Soviet shops were characterised by queuing and empty shelves.* In the late Seventies there had been a period of what was called détente: the Americans and Russians decided to make less threatening noises at each other for a change, even though they were still armed to the teeth.

In 1980, things began to change: a new American president was elected: Ronald Reagan. Reagan was a movie star (lower level) turned politician. He'd been governor of California and was a well-seasoned Republican, who'd lain in wait while Jimmy Carter muffed the Democrats' chance to show they were a viable alternative to the party that had put Richard Nixon into the White House.

---

* If you're a fan of the USSSRRRR then the queuing for shops with empty shelves simply underlines how they had got their priorities right: it's an argument, I guess.

Important Watergate sidebar

Watergate was the scandal that had brought Richard 'Tricky Dicky' Nixon down. If Vietnam was the American SUEZ squared then Watergate was like PROFUMO cubed but without the shagging and the Russians: lying galore, threadbare excuses and a suffix for the ages. The ins and outs of Watergate involved break-ins, bugging and Nixon taping himself because he didn't trust anyone. Long after all this was forgotten, -gate ended up the suffix that alerted the casual reader to the presence of a scandal.

Don't worry yourself with the details now: all you need to know is that Watergate, like Elvis or the Sex Pistols, looks remarkably un-shocking and weak beer by modern standards of political scandal. Don't know why he bothered stepping down. There was a time when Watergate was all some people would talk about to let you know they understood American politics, maybe bunging in a reference to Ted Kennedy and Chappaquiddick, but those days are gone and forgotten, as exciting as a Bakelite telephone now there are smartphones. Thank God. It used to be so tedious.

Ronald Reagan Free World Cold War cowboy renegade

Ronald Reagan had the air of man who wandered in off the street but, don't worry, he could handle the situation. Reagan had his own style of politics.

Reagan's reaction to the quadruple blow of American humiliation in Vietnam, the political squalor of Watergate, the economic fallout of the 1973 OPEC oil crisis and Carter's impotence in the face of the Iranian Revolution was to carry on as if none of those things really mattered. He'd style them out.

Reagan also decided that détente didn't really suit him; moreover it was his estimation that the Cold War was worth (not) fighting some more. He upped the rhetoric against the USRRRRR, and now that the US was well clear of Vietnam could do so without looking like a colossal hypocrite. He joked at press conferences about bombing Russia, which certainly didn't freak out everyone in Europe at the time. But at the same time, he felt he wanted to do something about disarming too, even as he ordered the next generation of world-ending gear.

However, changes were afoot in the USSSRRRRR and ones that ran to Reagan's advantage.

U.S. PRESIDENT

John F. Kennedy

Jack Kennedy – anything is possible, all you have to do is go for it, though don't look to closely at what I might be up to thanks

Lyndon B. Johnson

Lyndon B Johnson – look if someone has to do this goddam job it's me, I suppose, shut up!

Richard Nixon

Richard Nixon – what did you call my wife?

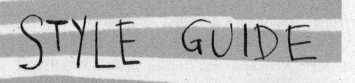

STYLE GUIDE

Gerald Ford

Jimmy Carter

Ronald Reagan

Gerald Ford – hell I don't know who I am either.

Jimmy Carter – gee, do you have to go off first impressions?

Ronald Reagan – well, if you will insist on me being President, this is what you're going to get.

Brezhnev Andropov Chernenko Gorbachev

Since Nikita Khrushchev had fumbled the CUBAN MISSILE CRISIS the Soviets had been under the leaden rule of Leonid Brezhnev. Brezhnev's USP was he was nowhere near as bad as STALIN, nowhere near as showy as Khrushchev. The Soviet Union settled into a plateau of icy Imperialism under Brezhnev: as the Sixties turned to the Seventies and the Soviets got left behind in the space race, the Politburo decreed that the Soviet Union should rest on its laurels and celebrate the Great Patriotic War. The Soviet Union may not yet have delivered the Workers' Paradise, but it had destroyed evil fascism, so you can grumble about Gulags and so on all you like but this system was what did for HITLER.

Things had become culturally and economically static, in contrast to the West's economic rollercoastering, TV and jeans – while in some of the Soviet satellite states, like East Germany (a.k.a. the DDR, one D for Deutschland, the other for Demokratische), things were grinding along with a heavy pinch of state surveillance and oppression. But you know, nobody's perfect.

The Soviet Union's leaders were all getting older and greyer and it was clear that pretty soon the baton was going to have to be passed to the post-Revolution generation. Mikhail Gorbachev was born in 1931 – his predecessor Chernenko, who led the USSRRR for a whole year, had been born in 1911. Gorbachev felt that the party had got stuck and that it was time to reform, shake things up, but in a Communist Party way: he was a Leninist after all. Lenin had been into reform, hadn't he? So Gorbachev decided that what the Soviet Union needed was openness – *glasnost* – and restructuring – *perestroika*. The problem was the Soviet state still wanted to keep its secrets – the souring war in Afghanistan had to be kept quiet and when the Chernobyl nuclear plant blew up* in April 1986, the urge to keep the insanely expensive catastrophe secret was overpowering.

At the same time, Ronald Reagan, never bothered about being confusing, had been upping the nuclear ante as well as offering to disarm. Gorbachev, who knew that the Cold War was an expensive habit he wanted the Soviet Union to break, jumped at the chance. By the end of the Eighties, the Effects of *glasnost* and *perestroika* were being felt – scrutiny of the Communist Party wasn't working well for it, and the stuff that had been done in the name of the Revolution was starting to be laid bare. A system that had relied on not telling anyone what was actually going on couldn't cope with people finding out what was actually going on. As he loosened the party's grip on private property, the whole thing started to unravel. The war in Afghanistan was given up for lost. By 1989, the Soviet Union was broke, both economically and politically.

---

* Technical term.

THE FALL OF THE BERLIN WALL, 1989

When Germany was cut in two in the aftermath of WER-WERTWO, the western bit became West Germany (FDR), the eastern part East Germany (DDR). So far so simple.

West Germany went on to be great at football and making cars, in a way that seemed personal if you were middle-aged and British in the 1970s.

It's fashionable, hip and, not only that, right to be rude about the DDR, so I'm going to try my best to be understanding.

East Germany, doing its best to deliver a Workers' Paradise, ended up in 1961 building what it called the Anti-Fascist Protection Rampart along the border between the two Germanies – the East German government said it was to keep West Germans out.* The wall had been built because three and a half million East Germans had left to go to West Germany, and the East German government didn't much want to end up without any

---

* YEAH, RIGHT!

Workers to deliver Paradise to, and when you put it like that the Berlin Wall seems entirely reasonable.

People would tunnel out of the East, smuggle themselves in fuel tanks, make a run for it, build gliders, or – and again this all makes sense from the point of view of the DDR government – sell citizens to the West as glorified hostages (the money kept things going, and every country needs exports). The Stasi, the DRR's secret police, kept tabs on everyone, recruiting people to spy on their neighbours, friends and families just to make sure they were all OK, probably. And to top it all, you couldn't get a pair of stone-washed jeans for love nor money.

The wall came to be symbolic of the difference between the West and the communist East, and unlike lots of things that are symbolic it didn't really require much interpretation. With watchtowers, minefields and patrolling dogs, it was really, really bad PR. American presidents *loved* the Berlin Wall: President Kennedy declared, 'Ich bin ein Berliner!'* though he made it quite clear he wouldn't do anything about the wall; Ronald Reagan echoed the sentiment. 'Mr Gorbachev,' he said, 'tear down this wall.' Even though really it made his job easier if he didn't.

For all the muttering about how it was nothing to do with the Soviet Union, it was Gorbachev who brought it down one way or another. The USSSRRRR's collapsing finances meant

---

* Setting off a half century of pedantry – German pedantry – about whether he'd actually described himself as a doughnut.

he had to pull the plug on East Germany, as well as the other states he'd been propping up.

Suddenly the COLD WAR, the Iron Curtain, the Eastern Bloc and all that came with it wasn't something that couldn't be challenged from within. People started crossing the border in their magnificent two-stroke Trabant cars. Gorbachev had broken the spell with help from David Bowie, Bruce Springsteen, Genesis and David Hasselhoff.* Unable to withstand the soft rock cultural onslaught, the Berlin Wall fell because an official hadn't made himself clear whether people could cross the border or not. On 9 November 1989, crowds pushed their way through the checkpoints to get into West Berlin and the next thing you knew it was all over: Berliners tore down the wall rather than Mr Gorbachev and that was that. Overnight the world changed. Now Germans could buy stone-washed jeans wherever they were.

Particularly clever people, most notably Francis Fukuyama, seemed to think somehow that this was 'the end of History'. But History had other ideas.

---

* Well, that's what Hasselhoff says, anyway.

THE *SATANIC VERSES* FATWA
ON SALMAN RUSHDIE, 1989

It is said in publishing that a signed book is a sold book: the same goes for burned books but people in publishing aren't as chirpy about it. Salman Rushdie, literary novelist (over the other side of the bookshop from here), wrote a novel called *The Satanic Verses* in which he did what people who write fiction do and made some stuff up. Not like this book, no ma'am.

However, the stuff he'd made up – although, obviously, he'd made it up – about the Prophet Muhammad, resulted in the Western world learning what a fatwa is. Although Rushdie's book was literary fiction, the sort that no one understands even if they do read it, it enraged the religious authorities in Iran, who announced he had blasphemed and declared they wanted him dead: a fatwa. There was a bounty on his head. Crowds gathered all over the world and denounced a book they hadn't read let alone understood. Rushdie went into hiding, doubtless as baffled as his readers.

This was all deadly serious: a Japanese translator of the book was murdered, bookshops were bombed, while at the same time some clever creative people seemed to suggest he should have known better, he had it coming and should have kept his mouth shut, a point of view that reflected well on no one.

Rushdie apologised, asked for the book not to be published: none of that worked.

In 1998, the Iranian government changed its mind and said it no longer required Rushdie dead, but the fatwa remains in place, adding another paradox to the whole thing. There's still a bounty in seven figures: almost three million dollars.

While in hiding, Rushdie managed to get married, appear on *Have I Got News for You* and in the end got a knighthood and a role in *Curb Your Enthusiasm*. Worth it.

NELSON MANDELA IS RELEASED, 1990

Nelson Mandela being released was like the fall of another BERLIN WALL, another one of those things that was symbolic and real at the same time.

MEANWHILE all this time since WERWERTWO, South Africa had drawn different conclusions about how bad HITLER had made racism look. By the time the dust had settled at the end of WERWERTWO, South Africa – who had been on the side of the Allies and therefore one of the good guys – decided that the best way to deal with race relations in the country was to do away with them altogether and institute Apartheid. The word means literally 'aparthood': the idea was that everyone would live apart in their own 'hoods.

Black and white were segregated; Asian and 'Coloureds' were also treated differently. Lots of idiotic racial theory went into this too. The big idea behind treating the vast majority of South Africa's population like dirt was to play off the two white populations in South Africa against each other and keep them happy: the Boer and the English. Black people were at

the bottom of the heap; they weren't allowed the vote and were restricted in the kind of work they could do. Piled on top of this jolly stinking constitutional dung heap was censorship and oppression of the medium-to-heavy fascist kind, with the occasional massacre to remind people of where they stood. You just beat the Nazis, you planks.

Resistance got started pretty quickly, as you might expect. The African National Congress organised and agitated against the Apartheid system and were committed to overthrowing the regime. The COLD WAR did its backdrop thing and the Soviets helped out the rebels – the South African government was sort of part of the West despite being in the south.

Nelson Mandela, along with many others, had been involved in protesting and agitating against the regime from the start. In 1956, Mandela had been on trial for treason for asserting the utterly insane and radical notion that South Africa belonged to everyone who lived there, black or white. He travelled the country disguised as a chauffeur – the press called him 'the Black Pimpernel'. In 1963, he was put on trial for sabotage: at the trial Mandela said yes, he had been doing some sabotage but had no intention of embarking on guerrilla warfare. That got him life. The struggle against Apartheid continued. Mandela faded from view.

By 1990, a lot had changed: except perhaps Mandela, who'd stuck it out in prison while Apartheid became more and more unsustainable, hanging on to his totally out-there message of South Africa belonging to everyone who lived there. On his release that year, it was clear that prison had driven him plain straight crazy when Mandela stunned the world by saying that really everyone in South Africa ought to be able to live in peace together, let bygones be bygones, and work together for once towards national harmony. The loony.

Mandela became president of South Africa and kept on his predecessor, F. W. de Klerk, the man who'd let him out, as his deputy. South Africa then became a beautiful homeland of peace, love and harmony ... I'll need to check this; it's been thirty years so it may not have all worked out the way he wanted it.

THE NEW WORLD ORDER IN THE 1990s: THE COLD WAR HAS ENDED, PEACE FOR ALL MANKIND

Before we get going on the era of peace and enlightenment that followed the end of the COLD WAR, it's worth brushing up on your historical Causes that explain in one simple cut-out-and-throw-away guide how things ended up the way they were in the 1990s.

- CAUSES OF COLD WAR FALLOUT: THE COLD WAR
- CAUSES OF THE COLD WAR: WERWERTWO
- CAUSES OF WERWERTWO: THE GREAT DEPRESSION
- CAUSES OF THE GREAT DEPRESSION: DOUBLEYOUDOUBLEYOU ONE
- CAUSES OF DOUBLEYOUDOUBLEYOU ONE: IMPERIALISM

So if you're feeling lazy, the simplest shortcut for all this is:

- CAUSES OF COLD WAR FALLOUT:
  IMPERIALISM. If you're in a rush, you can
  skip the others.

That's your A★ at A-level in the bag, trust me.

The 1990s were an era of new hope for a bright dawn for mankind unless you were paying any attention.

Let's get things started with Saddam Hussein reaping the peace dividend of the end of the COLD WAR by invading Kuwait.

THE GULF WAR, 1990–91

In 1990, the world got introduced to a new bad guy, though if you'd been paying attention you probably had some idea of who this exciting new moustachioed dictator was. Ba'ath Party supremo and uniformed tyrant Saddam Hussein had been minding his own business running a horrible state in Iraq, trying to play off both sides in the COLD WAR, as well as some genocide on the side against people who opposed him, like the Kurds murdered at Halabja in 1988. More importantly, he had been at war with Iran for most of the Eighties, a great long grim war that cost the lives of millions that no one seems to want to talk about. And this book is no exception.*

---

* Started in 1980, ran until 1988. 'Border disputes' between the two hard-boiled governments resulted in a draw, but a score draw, both sides claiming they had won. The conflict featured the use of chemical weapons, human wave attacks and deliberate targeting of civilians. Very hard to say how many died but probably more than a million in total. Iraqi men would turn up at the front with a coffin in anticipation of dying.

Author's note

Saddam Hussein was one of History's *bad men and villains* who was undeniably a *bad man and a villain*, it's just that as he did his *bad man villainy* on people who no one was that bothered about, he didn't make the papers that often.

Events

In 1990, Saddam Hussein decided he'd had enough of just being a regional menace and wanted to upgrade to the major leagues. The COLD WAR ending had changed everything – but this time, rather than picking on someone his own size, like he had with Iran, Saddam changed tack.

His war dead with Iran not yet cold in the grave, Saddam turned his attention to nearby Kuwait, one of those states in the Middle East that used to have petrol stations named after it. Kuwait had direct access to the Arabian Gulf, in the way that Iraq doesn't. He huffed and puffed, demanded hundreds of millions of dollars from Kuwait as reparations for being Kuwait, and invaded in August of 1990. I was on my summer holidays.

Causes? Imperialism, natch, but on this occasion it was on the part of Saddam Hussein's Iraq trying to sort itself an empire. **Depending on who you ask:** in which case it's Imperialism on the USA's part for, well, being the USA and I'll get back to you on the details, OK?

EFFECTS: an ongoing nightmare that is still with us today but that's current affairs/news not History.

The world looked on aghast once it figured out what was going on. US president George Bush (not that one, his dad) thought he was in for a quiet life with the COLD WAR having ended, and anyway, wasn't it Iran that had a beef with the US, not Iraq? It wasn't until TheThatcher told President Bush (no, his dad, I told you) to sort himself out and stand up to Iraqi aggression that he decided to act. TheThatcher, of course, had had a good war in the Falklands and could recommend the benefits of showing strength. By the time the war actually got started in January 1991, TheThatcher had been replaced by John Major, who in his dull, unflashy, reliable way agreed that war was the answer.

Also, America's oily ally Saudi Arabia felt threatened by Iraqi soldiers being next door in Kuwait. Which is fair enough. And the price of oil went up. Which is economics.

Only one thing for it: George Bush (no, not that one) assembled what he called a 'coalition of the willing' and demanded that Iraq get out of Kuwait immediately: 'This aggression will not stand,' he said, like in *The Big Lebowski*. With the COLD WAR ending, the USA was suddenly the only superpower in the world, and everything seemed so simple. Thirty-five countries joined in Bush's coalition (no, no, how many times?), ready to show the Iraqis who was boss, and for the first time *live on TV*.

CNN had reporters in Iraq 'embedded' with US forces, and you could watch it all day thanks to the innovation of twenty-four-hour news. This influenced public opinion enormously thanks to no one getting any sleep because they'd been up all night watching a war in a different time zone. There were weeks and weeks of build-up as the coalition got ready to retake Kuwait, unless Saddam changed his mind, which obviously he wasn't going to.

Operation Desert Storm – the British equivalent was called Operation Granby in an attempt to win a BAFTA for gritty realism – unleashed the American war machine, along with that of the other nations who'd been cajoled, persuaded, paid into turning up. The Iraqis had no answer to the high-tech assault. Cruise missiles flew into the Iraqi capital Baghdad on the news and massed tank armies swung into Iraq and took back Kuwait.

If Saddam Hussein was trying to get other people to kill Iraqis for him, he succeeded, in an incredibly one-sided contest. A hundred hours of combat saw the Iraqi army marmalised, as they say at staff college. Horrific pictures of the road to Basra, where the retreating Iraqis had got caught and were being attacked by the coalition's air forces, underlined how uneven the whole thing had been.

At the time, President Bush (I've told you, not that one, his dad) decided that what he couldn't do was go all the way to Baghdad and overthrow Saddam Hussein: after all, the UN had specified liberating Kuwait and nothing else.

President Bush (look, drop it, OK?) had spent a lot of time comparing Saddam to HITLER (in proper HITLER HITLER HITLER style) and although Saddam didn't exactly have global domination on his mind, more a bigger stake in the world's oil supply,* where he was similar to HITLER was that even seeing his armies destroyed *live on TV* didn't make him throw in the towel.

Outcome

- Iraq remained under a 'no-fly' zone – the Iraqi air force was forbidden from flying its planes.
- Iraqi Kurds were allowed to govern their own region.
- A win for George Bush (what is your problem?), though he then went on to lose the next election.
- Bush (shh, now) proclaimed a 'New World Order' which lasted the historical equivalent of a nanosecond.
- Saddam Hussein stayed put as Iraqi dictator until he ran into, of all people, George Bush (yes, that one, happy now?).

---

* Same difference, ran the argument.

Conclusion: frozen soup

TROUBLE IN IRAQ BEING STORED UP FOR LATER LIKE
FROZEN SOUP READY TO BE REHEATED IN THE EVENT
OF AN EMERGENCY/POWER CUT.

THE YUGOSLAV WARS

In further COLD WAR-ending-outbreak-of-peace events we have the Yugoslav Wars. In which the cobbled-together multi-ethnic state of Yugoslavia fell apart horribly, having previously been held together with a delightful combo of tough-guy dictator Tito's personal grip and a dash of not-quite-Stalinist COMMUNISM.* Tito had fallen out with STALIN when the COLD WAR began, wanting to do things his way.

Yugoslavia (don't look for it on the map, it isn't there any more) was made up of countries and provinces in the Balkans left over from the fall of the Austro-Hungarian Empire. Founded in 1918 as soon as DOUBLEYOUDOUBLEYOU ONE ended, it consisted of Bosnia and Herzegovina, Croatia, Kosovo, Montenegro, North Macedonia, Serbia and Slovenia. Like a lot of the new countries that followed the TREATY OF VERSAILLES, it required a balancing act for the Yugoslav

---

* This is a precis, by the way, remember that at all times. But just because it's a precis doesn't mean it's wrong.

government with lots of different ethnic groups and powerful factions pulling in different directions.

It's complicated, OK?

During WERWERTWO, Yugoslavia had been invaded by the Germans. Some people had picked sides during the war. It's complicated. Really complicated. The kind of complicated that were it a tangled set of headphones, you'd sooner bin it than try to unravel it.

Tito kept a lid on things until his death in 1980. During the Eighties, tensions between the different parts of Yugoslavia grew, and these tensions were mainly around how best to rule a country made up of lots of different peoples when one of those peoples – the Serbs – were very much in the majority, and held many of the top jobs throughout the country. On the face of it, the Serbs were trying to keep the old communist state going. As the different nationalities tried to make sure they were properly represented in a complicated national way, complications ensued. Complicatedly. It began to become clear that making a multiethnic state out of lots of people who really hated each other might not be such a brilliant idea.

As the Eighties became the Nineties and the dawn of new hope spread its post-COLD WAR rays of beautiful peace, the Yugoslav state began to fall apart. The Serbs in the majority used the Yugoslav army to try to stop different bits of the country leaving, or seceding. Slovenia was the first to go: in 1991 there was an incident called the Ten-Day War, which Slovenia won, successfully leaving Yugoslavia. That was it, war over. Until that same year it got more complicated.

Croatia also decided it had had enough and was going to leave Serb-dominated Yugoslavia: it prepared to secede. Then Serbs within Croatia decided that they wanted to secede from seceding Croatia. Fighting followed. The Yugoslav army (read Serbian) came to the rescue of the Croatian Serbs, the seceding anti-secessionists.

There were massacres too: they weren't complicated. They were simply people being murdered in what was called 'ethnic cleansing'. 'Ethnic cleansing' was meant to sound like a euphemism but was no such thing. It became clear that the Serbian leadership were keen on creating something called Greater Serbia. Greater in this instance meant bigger. While it started out saying that what it was doing was holding Yugoslavia together, it became evident that what Serbian leader Slobodan Miloševiç meant was Serbians.

Further complications: Bosnia gets the independence bug

When Bosnia declared independence in 1992, things didn't so much go up a gear as switch to a much bigger vehicle. In Bosnia there were also Serbs who wanted to stay part of Yugoslavia. Sarajevo – where the story of *The Last Hundred*

Years (Give or Take) and All That started – was besieged for three years, ten months and three weeks. It perhaps tells you how far things had changed since 1914 that the world didn't go to war over what was happening in the Balkans. Or at least not yet it didn't.

In the ethnic mix, Bosnia and Herzegovina was full of Bosniaks or Bosnian Muslims. These Muslims were the target of 'ethnic cleansing'. Massacre upon massacre followed in a way that hadn't been seen since WERWERTWO, which people liked to say had been fought to stop exactly this sort of thing. In July 1995, more than 8,000 Bosnian Muslims were murdered – men and boys mainly, on the grounds that they were Bosnian Muslim men and boys.

The international community

As the multiple civil wars unfolded, the international community – which makes it sound like there's a youth centre where they meet and drink squash from plastic beakers – decided the best thing to do was say, 'Oh gosh no, please stop it.' Despite the gung-ho attitude to kicking Iraq out of Kuwait, it was quickly acknowledged that the Yugoslavian civil wars were:

1. None of anyone's business;
2. Really, really complicated;
3. Just too bad;

4. You couldn't say something must be done because then you might have to do something;
5. Look what happened last time Europe got overexcited about the Balkans;
6. Oh my, isn't it terrible?

UN peacekeepers did everything they could to not get involved, making the UN look like it cared enough to turn up, but not enough to do anything about what was happening, like a fireman without a hose.

In the meantime, the plight of the Bosniaks attracted the attention of fellow Muslims, and donors from all over the Islamic world sorted out their co-religionists with weapons and grumbled about how the West did nothing. No way whatsoever that attitude would mutate into something far, far more dangerous.

By mid-1995, the Americans had managed to get some of the warring parties to the table, but in Bosnia they'd not got far. It was a mark of their success that NATO started bombing Bosnian Serb positions and equipment in August 1995, forcing a ceasefire and a negotiated peace by the end of the year. A chunk of Bosnia became the Republic of Srpska for Serbs to live in and the fighting ended. At least in Bosnia and Herzegovina.

What do you mean there's more?

In the manner of a TV show that went on for one series too many, the war carried on.

Kosovo was the last of the Yugoslav territories to secede. In 1996, when you might think Serbia had got the message that the whole of the rest of the country wanted to unfriend it, there had been a brief uprising. In 1998, things kicked off properly; NATO brokered a peace that fell apart at the start of 1999. Rather than wait, NATO – on chipmunk evangelist Tony Blair*'s urging – sent in a peacekeeping force with James Blunt on guitar.† As if that wasn't persuasive enough, NATO also bombed Serbia itself to prevent it being able to do anything out of line in Kosovo, though at the same time they bombed the Chinese Embassy by accident but best not dwell on that, eh?

---

* IRAQ!

† Nice bloke actually. Don't really see why he annoys people quite so much. And if his sweet acoustic guitar of peace isn't to your taste, just whose side are you on?

Aftermath

The Yugoslav Wars resulted in the end of Yugoslavia, war crime trials at the Hague for the main Serbian players and a decade-long hiatus of the dinner-party conversation about how you really must charter a yacht on the Croatian coast.

LESSONS FROM HISTORY

1. If you really do have to build a country out of the remains of someone's dead empire, have a good think about whether the people who live in those remains can stand the sight of each other. Often as not, once you remove the empire they all hate from the picture they just get on with hating each other.
2. If someone says they're going to do 'ethnic cleansing', best take them at their word.

Which leads us to:

THE RWANDAN GENOCIDE

Causes

Imperialism.* Racism.† A civil war that turned genocidal.‡ A country made up of different ethnic groups that really couldn't stand each other, and were encouraged to hate each other.§ The UN biting its lip and doing nothing.¶ An assassination used as an excuse for political insurrection.** How many times can you tell this story, you might be wondering?

---

* You know it!

† No matter how bad racists make racism look, people just keep on falling for it.

‡ Oh my. It's happening again.

§ Cause: Imperialism! 10/10

¶ Stop me if you've heard this one before.

** The old tunes are the best.

Background: e.g. where is Rwanda for a start?

Rwanda had been created during the nineteenth century, like large chunks of Africa, as an African country with a border that didn't take into account who lived there.

Rwanda, bordered on the south by Burundi from which it was split when it gained independence, lies to the east of the Democratic Republic of the Congo, next door to Uganda to its north and Tanzania to its east. You still don't know where it is. Admit it.

The hangover from the country's History as a German and then a Belgian colony was the racial dimension to its politics. Hutus and Tutsis, two of the different ethnic groups organised in clans, had been defined as races, the Tutsis deemed superior because of their longer noses or necks. Which was the kind of thing that sounded reasonable to racists. This was baked in by identity cards that the Belgians insisted were carried, identifying the bearer's race. Hutus responded to this favouritism by hating Tutsis rather than Belgians. A third group, the Twa, were caught in the middle. Independence switched the balance – the Belgians had changed their mind as to which group they preferred – so the Hutus were in charge, but racial violence was never far from the surface.

Fan meet shit

By the Nineties, a post-post-colonial civil war was underway. Hutus and Tutsis had been fighting since independence from Belgium in the late Fifties. The civil war in 1990 was started by a group of exiled Tutsis, the Rwandan Patriotic Front, invading, trying to get back into Rwanda because why wouldn't you want to go back to a country that wanted you dead? The civil war was deadlocked; the RPF's demands were simple but in the context of the country's racists politics totally out there: stop treating Tutsis as second-class citizens, grant their return, treat them like people. Y'know, call me a bleeding heart but it doesn't sound that mad.

The Rwandan government tried to strike a peace deal with the RPF, but long-term Rwandan president Juvénal Habyarimana found he couldn't satisfy anyone. Hutu, government and army discontent about the deal he'd done went underground, and planning began to kill as many Tutsis as possible from about 1992. When the president's plane was shot down – and it remains disputed whether it was his own side that did it or the RPF – on 6 April 1994, Rwanda immediately erupted into genocide, the government that succeeded Habyarimana 100 per cent behind the slaughter. The army had already handed out machetes; Hutu kids had been trained and encouraged to kill Tutsis. Radio messages urging Hutus to kill Tutsis were broadcast.

The genocide lasted months, during which time the UN did its fireman without a hose thing, and the world looked on in horror and shock – it's not like anyone had heard of Rwanda except maybe in Belgium where the whole thing was something of an embarrassment. As many as a million Tutsis were murdered, as well as 'politically moderate' Hutus, which you can take to mean Hutus who didn't think Tutsis should be killed because of who they were.

The RPF resumed the civil war when the killings began, and gradually beat the government forces, overthrowing the Hutu establishment but seeking justice and reconciliation instead of revenge. Two million Hutus had fled the way you might depart from the scene of the crime. Rwanda has the dull distinction of being half-remembered and renowned for a genocide that no one knows much about anyway, not unlike Cambodia.

HONG KONG: PHOOEY

The lease on Hong Kong – for it was a lease – ran out in 1997. Usually when a lease runs out it means you rush around trying to get the Blu-Tack off the walls, fix the toilet that hasn't flushed properly for 18 months. However, this was a little different. Hong Kong had first been colonised by the British in 1842, bit by bit the lease was extended.

- In 1899 When Britain had took the 98-year lease on Hong Kong: it was a global superpower, ruthless in the application of force to getting its way.
- China: was a basket case.
- In 1997 when the lease ran out: I'll leave the rest to you.

A hundred and fifty-six years of British rule was over. Chinese rule was on. Hong Kong, however, benefited from being a money-making machine, through manufacturing, shipping and trading. China, not yet the world's workshop for everything, wanted the injection of cash and probably, though it's hard to discern the extent to which the Chinese Communist Party cared, the chance to look law-abiding and street-legal. What with the events that definitely didn't happen in Tiananmen Square in 1989 that no one mentioned no ma'am, as well the world's biggest army, this was no normal end of lease 'what do you mean you've burned the carpet?' inventory situation.

Negotiations followed, though what there was to negotiate was something worth pondering: the British government couldn't exactly stop the Chinese government from doing what it wanted. TheThatcher baulked at giving everyone in Hong Kong a passport. John Major's government sent Chris Patten to be the last governor of Hong Kong. This was unusual – Patten was a politician rather than a diplomat and got on with enacting last-minute democratic reforms in Hong Kong because, well, you would, wouldn't you? One final yank of the tiger's tail. PUB QUIZ FACT: his nickname was Fatty Pang.

The handover came at midnight on 1 July 1997. A huge ceremony with endless Chinese soldiers and parades of important politicians as well as Prince Charles marked the end of the British Empire.* Charles read a farewell message from the Queen, Tony Blair† looked on and Chris Patten sweated into his ill-fitting suit.

It was probably the last time anyone wore a pith helmet and

---

* Imperialism.
† IRAQ!

not as fancy dress. That's History.

Hong Kong then carried on as before except totally different: what they called the 'One country, two systems' approach, though as of writing, well, God knows how that's going to end up.

For red-faced blokes all over the world, the effect of change in Hong Kong will be felt when they cancel the rugby sevens.

THE FORMATION OF
THE PREMIER LEAGUE

Until this fateful date of 20 February 1992, all anyone could hope for in football was the Football League First Division. With a stroke of the administrative pen, the twenty top clubs broke away and formed the greatest football league ever in the History of football leagues globally and of all time: the Premier League, which means 'first'. Known as the EPL all over the world, the Premier League is the league all other leagues aspire to be.

At the time there were dire warnings and grim predictions that what would happen is the top five or six clubs would end up super-clubs, hoovering up money and players from all over the world, forcing the other clubs that couldn't compete financially into a state of permanent second-class stasis, while being relegated could prove ruinous. Luckily, none of that happened.

Origins

TV supremo Greg Dyke wanted to get his hands on all the top games for London Weekend Television (don't look for it, it's not there any more). Now it's on Sky and BT Sport. That's History.

THE CHANNEL TUNNEL

Before TheThatcher was thrown out of government by the rest of the Tory Party for not liking Europe enough – long story best left; as ever it involved TheThatcher driving everyone mad – she had made plans for the inviolate island of Great Britain to be connected permanently to Europe by means of a tunnel to France.

For a long time until TheThatcherYears, a tunnel under the Channel had been the exclusive domain of mad dreamers and speculators. In 1981, TheThatcher and the French president, François Mitterrand, changed all that, and commissioned a report on a privately funded Channel Tunnel.

TheThatcher expected the tunnel to be just cars but the French wanted passenger trains and freight – a more ambitious project and the one that was settled on in the end. After the kind of wrangling you might expect with at least two sets of builders – one British, one French – and two governments involved, work began in 1988: boring from both sides (do your own jokes).

The French boring machines were named after women; the British machines were given names with letters and numbers, settling once and for all which country is sexier.

In 1990, the service tunnels met in the middle. In 1994, services began, the tunnel massively over budget and basically bankrupt but you could get from London to Paris in less time than it took you to get to Edinburgh.

The Channel Tunnel is an engineering wonder of the world but because it wasn't built by a man in a stovepipe hat no one cares about it. And it's nowhere near as much fun as a cross-Channel ferry with a Space Invaders machine.

NEW LABOUR, NEW DANGER

In 1997, the Labour Party, which had been out of government since 1979, blocked at every turn by the TheThatcher's
country-blasting style of pretending to be inflexible while also
making it up as she went along combined with sheer bloody
luck, finally won a general election.

In 1992, John Major, who seemed nice enough and by
today's standards gives the impression of being both sane
and competent, beat Labour leader Neil Kinnock to Number
10. Kinnock, a.k.a. 'the Welsh Windbag' on account of his
fondness for playing specially adapted Welsh bagpipes, had
done all he could to try to get the Labour Party to the point
where it might win an election, but the 1992 electorate had
opted for the Devil It Knew in the form of the dull, reliable
and honestly-if-you're-not-careful-you'll-end-up-wishing-there-
were-more-of-him-about, Mr Major.

John Major – and believe me this is more complicated
than (German hyperinflation x YUGOSLAV WARS) – crashed
his government's reputation for being good at economics by

leaving the European Exchange Rate Mechanism. On Black Wednesday – 16 September 1992 – the pound was forced out of the ERM and economic chaos ensued: interest rates went bananas and the housing market crashed. From then on, Major's Tory government looked daft and compromised, not helped by the MPs in the Conservative Party who were still keen to show how mad TheThatcher had driven them by arguing over Europe all the time in the manner of the one-eyed All Blacks fan, and in some cases perjuring themselves and asking questions in Parliament for cash and not being that bothered who knew it. 'Tory sleaze' they called it, because it was sleaze, and it was Tory.

What's in a name? John Smith

In the wake of the 1992 election, Kinnock was replaced by John Smith, who was neither Welsh, nor a windbag. Instead he was a dour Scottish lawyer, the kind you might want representing you if you'd been caught streaking. In a national dull-off (remember, we like dull, dull is good!), Labour clawed back some of its hard-lost respectability. The main weapon in Smith's arsenal was not being Welsh. It looked like being Scottish was the way forward.

But things never have been easy for the Labour Party: in 1994, Smith died of a heart attack.

The search was on for a new Scottish Labour Party leader.

Two men were in the frame more than any others: Gordon Brown, self-styled intellectual heavyweight and gurning deep thinker, and the earnest leisure-centre-manager-charisma'd Tony Blair*. Both were Scots, both essentially humourless and Messianic, but Blair deployed the electorally inspired card of appearing not to be Scottish at all. It worked, to the point where even Scots deny, to this day, that Blair was ever Scottish. Nothing to do wi' us, pal.

While the Tories imploded, exploded, reploded, deploded, outploded, byploded, underploded, overploded, Tony Blair† went around shaking people by the hand and looking them in the eye a tiny bit too sincerely and chipped away at the Tories, saying things like, 'Education, education, education,' as if he were trying to hypnotise you into robbing a bank for a Channel 4 show.

Blair did everything he could to make Labour look different, even – and believe it or not this worked – changing the name a bit, to New Labour. The Big Thing that Blair did was ditch Clause 4 of the Labour Party's constitution, which committed it to public ownership of stuff: to some this was a sign he'd gone full Tory and was yet another victim of TheThatcher's insanity powers, to others a sign that the times had changed and Labour was moving with them. The team around him, electoral guru Peter Mandelson and shouting expert Alastair Campbell,

---

* IRAQ!
† IRAQ!

made sure that the Labour Party stayed on message, behaved and didn't blow it this time, for Christ's sake what is wrong with you, why are you going on about the Jarrow March and Nicaragua for heaven's sake?

Come the 1997 election – which John Major had put off until the last minute in the hope that something would come up – the Labour Party smashed through with a historic landslide, exceeding all expectations and sweeping the Tories away all over the country. No one was more surprised than Tony Blair* who spent the next couple of years wandering around in a daze.

TONY BLAIR ELECTION QUIZ –
SHOW YOUR WORKING

a) Tony Blair† said he would be tough on what, tough on the Causes of what?

b) Complete the following: 'Education, education ...'

c) 'Things Can Only Get Better' by the band D:Ream was the anthem of the New Labour campaign in 1997. What things did get better?

d) Who won the 1997 election for Labour: Peter Mandelson and Alastair Campbell or 'cash for questions'-Tory-sleaze-personified Neil Hamilton?

---

* IRAQ!
† IRAQ!

The New Labour government embarked on a series of bright ideas and reforms that the Major government couldn't have begun to contemplate; though it kept on some of the ideas that Major and his crew had had, such as the Millennium Dome – a great big tent thing that cost far more than expected and was filled with an exhibition that an earnest leisure centre manager would approve of.

CANDLE IN THE WIND, 1997

On the last day of August 1997, the world came to a halt with the news that Princess Diana and her boyfriend Dodi Al Fayed had been killed in a car crash in Paris.

Princess Diana's world-famously unhappy marriage to Prince Charles had ended in divorce: she spent her newfound freedom being chased around by paparazzi keen on a snap of her with whoever she was – as they said – 'romantically involved'.*

Diana would sometimes court the press – giving exclusive interviews on the telly and saying there were three people in her marriage, that kind of thing, and other times she would go and stand in a minefield in a not altogether subtle attempt to make them go away.

Princess Diana's death was a huge shock. Henri Paul, who was driving her car, was drunk. She wasn't wearing a seatbelt. She was thirty-six. Her sons, Princes Harry and William, were little kids, not goofy adults trying to be as right-on as possible.

---

* Shagging.

The UK was plunged into mourning the likes of which had never been seen before. Tony Blair* described her as 'the people's princess' and he did it with a straight face, too. Everything happened in a mad tumble: crowds gathered, grown men wept in the street, the Queen ended up having to make an address to the nation to 'show us you care, Ma'am'. At the funeral, Diana's brother tried to settle scores somehow, Elton John sang 'Goodbye England's Rose' and people clapped the coffin on its way up the M1.

This historian was left entirely Baffled By The Whole Thing, though those members of the public who were Baffled By The Whole Thing also thought How Awful It All Was For Her Children. Because it was Awful For Her Children.

As the moment receded, the nutjobs, idiots, fruits and loons got cracking on it and soon enough Princess Diana hadn't died because a drunk driver lost control of her car and she wasn't wearing a seatbelt, but because MI6, Mossad, the SAS and Prince Philip had used an anti-matter gun to bombard her car with tiny Fiat Unos which blinded the (drunk) driver who was working for the secret service add your own favourite conspiracy to the mix and simmer on message boards for more than twenty years. Because as this book has demonstrated time and again, the most simple explanation is never quite enough.

---

* IRAQ!

THE GOOD FRIDAY AGREEMENT, 1998

WARNING: THE AUTHOR HAS LIVED HIS ENTIRE LIFE
IN WHAT'S CALLED 'THE MAINLAND' BY PEOPLE WHO
SHOULD KNOW BETTER – INCLUDING THE AUTHOR
– SO THIS NEXT SECTION ON NORTHERN IRISH POLI-
TICS IS PROBABLY INSULTINGLY BRIEF BUT I DON'T
WANT TO LET ANYONE DOWN NOW, DO I?

Given the religious-based sectarian political strife that had
plagued Northern Ireland for decades you'd be forgiven for
thinking that getting everyone in Ulster to agree when Good
Friday was would be an uphill battle in itself.

Attempts to get the many myriad hatchets buried in Northern
Ireland had been going on since the 1970s – with varying degrees
of success, possibly hindered by the IRA blowing up the Grand
Hotel in Brighton in a near-miss attempt to kill TheThatcher and
her Cabinet. Her successor John Major started talks with the IRA,
aimed at getting them to give up violence. The IRA agreed to a
ceasefire in 1994, which lasted three years, but they'd made the

mistake of showing that they could do it and what peace might be like. Rule One of armed struggle: never show what it's like when the shooting stops. Everyone prefers it.

Tony Blair picked up where John Major left off and pursued peace. Sinn Féin, the IRA's political 'wing', which makes it sound like a mental hospital, had made a prolonged effort to go legit and not speak for the IRA. A major bone of contention – a diplodocus's-rib-sized bone – was what the IRA might do with its weapons in the event of peace, something the British army never had to contemplate. That's probably what caused the hold-up. IRA spokesman Gerry Adams and 'hardman' Martin McGuinness, underwent the transformation into normal politicians and the unbelievable happened when they sat down to talk with loyalist Reverend Ian Paisley, who usually preferred shouting.

Tony Blair* involved the Irish government in the peace process. All concerned parties (and parties in Northern Ireland are always concerned) met in Northern Ireland, along with US president and planetary super-shagger Bill Clinton, who did what Americans do and came to Ireland claiming to be Irish, shaking hands with everyone and spending like a sailor on shore leave. It was a winning combo, and on Good Friday, 10 April 1998, the British and Irish governments signed the Good Friday Agreement.

Various Republican splinter groups tried to disrupt the peace process, most notably the Real IRA who killed scores of people

---

* IRAQ!

in Omagh in August 1998. But the peace genie was out of the bottle and now in Northern Ireland the bones of contention are gay cakes and divots with flags.

THE CENTURY, NAY, THE MILLENNIUM ENDS

His time in office seemed to get to Tony Blair[*]: the climax to the century came when Tony Blair[†], to celebrate the arrival of the Millennium on the 31 December 1999, tried to set fire to the River Thames while the Queen pulled a face that spoke for a nation.

---

[*] IRAQ!
[†] IRAQ!

THE LAST TWENTY YEARS
AND ALL THAT:
21st-CENTURY FANCY DRESS

And here we are in 2020 dear student, a year that will on its own fill countless History books; 2020 is going to get its own row in the History books bit of your local bookshop come 2120. Thrill at the prospect, dear reader.

We are living in a History book right now and I don't know about you but it isn't that much fun. Perhaps that is the BEST WAY to figure out how on earth it might have felt during the Great Depression or the Cuban Missile Crisis. Historians of the future will dissect this momentous year as if it were a frog, and probably declare it a toad. Such is the peril of the student of History.

Who knows what they will say, what conclusions they'll draw and who will have got their version of events down first. For all we know President Trump might be viewed in the way JFK is now, a shining example in his turbulent times, a true representative of his people and country.

But the thing they always say about History of course, is that it doesn't repeat itself. No way. How could it? Circumstances are always different, and as you know from this book, and the deeper you dig, Causes and Effects reveal themselves in a myriad of different ways.

So maybe rather than repeating itself, perhaps what's happening, is the twenty-first century is doing some Twentieth Century cosplay, like a lonely geek trying to make friends at the weekend. Trying on some of the highlights from *The Last Hundred Years and All That* for size and seeing if our bum looks big in them.

This cosplay as the previous century is being done in a random mix and match fashion, without due regard for the dates* or the order things happened in, rather with a taste for the overall retro vibe. It's that or we've all watched too many documentaries about the Twentieth Century and don't know how else to behave.

Since 1999, the world has done everything it can to dress up as the previous century: kicking off with terrorist murder that set in motion a global chain of events, followed by a big, apparently pointless war that inadvertently changed everything. Bin Laden and his pals' Gavrilo Princip costumes certainly got everyone's attention; not least George W. Bush, who got to do two cosplays for the price of one, taking on a moustachioed dictator – Saddam Hussein offering the world his Hitler–Stalin

---

* And I said, don't sweat the dates, didn't I?

– and doing his best impression of his own father by screwing up in the Middle East big time. Tony Blair* did cosplay Margaret Thatcher–Winston Churchill though without anyone willing to offer their Arthur Scargill. No one knows who Gordon Brown came as, but it frightened children, old ladies, everyone else.

Then the global economy, not to be outdone by the politicians and their creepy outfits, went full-on economic boom followed by full-on economic bust, making the Great Depression look positively homeopathic. Coupled with, of course, an American president who doesn't know his posterior from his humerus – *plus* a global pandemic bang on schedule for the anniversary of the SPANISH FLU. Which inevitably in the UK is being treated as a rerun of the Blitz/Battle of Britain. PLUS! Brexit, which is also being treated as a rerun of the Blitz/Battle of Britain.

In fact it's a safe bet that anything happening in the UK in the early to mid twenty-first century will be treated as a rerun of the Blitz/Battle of Britain and anyone you disagree with is cosplaying Hitler. In Russia, Vladimir Putin is cosplaying absolutely everyone you can think of from *The Last Hundred Years And All That* all at once and he is having a ball.

The twenty-first century is a fancy-dress party at a comic convention and no one is having any fun.

In this volume we have seen many excellent and pertinent **LESSONS FROM HISTORY**, as well as ignored a bunch of others,

---

* IRAQ!

possibly because they are too depressing/embarrassing. And this is what *The last Hundred Years And All That* can teach us perhaps, always keep

1. your head down,
2. your hopes up,

and a spare set of underwear and socks somewhere about your person.

ACKNOWLEDGEMENTS

This book was born, spawned and formed in lockdown. Whether lockdown is a good place to write: well you can be the judge of that, dear reader. Yet even though I saw no one else involved in this tome's creation, I should thank them anyway even though it's essentially all my fault: Jane Sturrock and Charlotte Fry, Hannah Cawse and Dom Gribben, Hannah Robinson, Bethan Ferguson and Hannah Winter, Sophia Surjadi and Dan Lloyd, Yusef Osman, Katie McKay and Richard Allen Turner. I'd also like to thank Tony Pastor, Harry, Jon and Joey at the We Have Ways team for enthusiasm and stimulus this summer, as well as the peerless James Holland. And of course all my love and thanks to the family: ESWD&C xxx